J. Radford Thomson

Guide to the District of Craven and the Settle and Carlisle Railway

J. Radford Thomson

Guide to the District of Craven and the Settle and Carlisle Railway

ISBN/EAN: 9783337059934

Printed in Europe, USA, Canada, Australia, Japan

Cover: Foto ©ninafisch / pixelio.de

More available books at **www.hansebooks.com**

GUIDE

TO THE DISTRICT OF

CRAVEN

AND THE

Settle and Carlisle Railway,

(WITH ILLUSTRATIONS.)

BY

J. RADFORD THOMSON, M.A.

SECOND EDITION.

LONDON:
SIMPKIN, MARSHALL, AND CO.; FREDERICK WARNE & CO.
SETTLE: HENRY GORE.

1879.

₊ *If any difficulty is experienced in obtaining this Guide, a copy will be forwarded direct from the Publisher for Twenty stamps.*

PREFACE.

THE Publisher, having for some years past received almost daily applications for a GUIDE BOOK TO CRAVEN, and being unable to meet the demand of the public, has asked me to prepare a manual for the use of Tourists, who, in yearly increasing numbers, resort to this attractive and interesting part of Yorkshire. And, as the opening of the Railway from Settle to Carlisle—the Midland Company's new route to Scotland—has brought a district formerly little known within the range of the ordinary tourist, it seemed a suitable occasion to provide a handbook to a part of the country, singularly wild, romantic, and interesting. The position of Settle, in the very heart of Craven, and at the point of departure of the new railroad, suggested that a description of the region penetrated by that remarkable line might appropriately be included in this volume.

Although I have myself explored all the more important of the localities I have described I cheerfully acknowledge obligations to many fellow-labourers in this department of Topography.

I have made free use of the observations and researches of the late Mr. WILLIAM HOWSON, whose "Illustrated Guide to the Curiosities of Craven," published in 1850, has for some years been out of print. As a native and a resident, Mr. Howson had opportunities for acquainting himself with Craven, which he diligently used, and as a geologist and an antiquarian he was highly qualified for the task he fulfilled.

It need scarcely be said that I am largely indebted to Dr. WHITAKER'S "History of Craven," and to Prof. PHILLIPS's "Rivers, Mountains, and Sea-coast of Yorkshire."

In preparing that part of this "Guide" which relates to the new line of railway, I have been largely assisted by the painstaking, comprehensive, and interesting work of my friend, Mr. F. WILLIAMS, upon "The Midland Railway, its Rise and Progress." Use has also been made of SAYERS' "History of Westmorland," and JEFFERSON's "History and Antiquities of Leith Ward."

I have also found sundry books of home travel of considerable service. I would especially mention Mr. W. WHITE's "Month in Yorkshire," Mr. W. DOBSON's "Rambles by the Ribble," Mr. W. S. BANKS's "Walks in Yorkshire," Mr. B. J. HARKER's "Rambles in Upper Wharfedale," and Mr. J. CARR's "Rambles about Ingleton."

Information has in some places been derived from MURRAY's and BLACK's "Guides to Yorkshire."

Chapters xiii, xiv, and xv have been reprinted from Howson's guide with additions and alterations.

The district of Craven has long been celebrated amongst Botanists for its production of a great variety of interesting plants. A capital handbook to these will be found in Dr. WATTS' "School Flora," a book which will be found extremely useful by all who have mastered the elements of botanical science. The late Dr. WINDSOR of Manchester compiled a "Flora Cravoniensis," which shows how thoroughly he had explored every nook and cranny of the district surrounding Settle. Unfortunately it has only been printed for private circulation, but the local publisher of this Guide will be glad to favour any enthusiastic Botanist with the loan of a copy.

In describing the country bordering the Settle and Carlisle Railway, I have made use of some articles, which I contributed to the "SHEFFIELD AND ROTHERHAM INDEPENDENT.'

It only remains to add, that, for the sake of variety and vivacity, I have, in some portions of the book, written in the first person plural. In a "Guide," which is a *vade mecum* rather than a topographical treatise, this liberty will perhaps be pardoned.   J. R. T.

CONTENTS.

	CHAP.
Description of Craven and its railway communications...	I.
Skipton	II.
Ilkley, Bolton, and Upper Wharfedale	III.
Malham and Gordale	IV.
Settle and Giggleswick	V.
Scaleber, Attermire, and the Victoria Cave	VI.
Clapham and Ingleborough Cave	VII.
Ingleton, Chapel-le-dale, and Kingsdale	VIII.
The lower Ribblesdale	IX.
The Settle and Carlisle Railway	X.
Upper Ribblesdale, Denthead, and Hawes	XI.
The Eden Valley	XII.
Geology of Craven	XIII.
Botany of Craven	XIV.
Dialect of Craven	XV.

INDEX.

Addingham 23, 109
Aire, source of..................... 41
Ais Gill Moor 87
Airton 38
Amerdale 35
Austwick 61, 62
Appleby   11, 15, 89, 97, 102—106
Appleby Church & Castle... 104, 105
Appletreewick 31
Armathwaite 90, 109
Arncliffe 35
Arten Ghyll 86
Attermire 45, 54, 55
Attermire Rocks 10
Barden Fells 10, 24, 32
Barden Tower 28, 30
Barnoldswick............... 55, 74, 75
Batty Green 85
Batty Moss 71
Batty Moss Viaduct............... 85
Battle Barrow Bank 89
Beckermonds 36
Bell Busk and Railway Station 38
Ben Rhydding..................... 22
Bingley 11
Birkett Tunnel......... 87, 88, 101
Bishopdale 36
Black Foss....................... 96
Blea Moor 85, 95
Bolton .... 21, 22—29
Bolton Abbey 24, 26, 27, 33
Bolton Woods and Strid...... 24, 28
Bolton Hall 26
Bolton-by-Bowland 74, 76
Bowland or Bolland Forest ... 78
Bowder Stones..................... 62
Botany of Craven 120
Breadagarth 72
Browsholme Hall 78
Bracewell..................... 74, 77
Broughton Hall 74
Brow Gill......................... 95, 96
Buckden 36
Buckden Pike 10, 36
Buckhaw Brow 51, 66
Burley........................... 21
Burnsall 32
Carlisle 10, 11, 91

Castle Hough 75
Castleberg......................... 45, 47
Cam Fell 10, 32, 37, 82, 95
Cat Knot Hole 95
Cautley Spout 96
Calton Hall 38
Catterick or Catrigg Foss 52
Cattle, Wild (Gisburne Park) 75
Chaucer quoted... 36
Chapel-le-dale......... 34, 66, 69, 95
Clapham and Cave 45, 61, 65
Clifford Family .... 15—19
Clifford, Lady Anne 100, 109
Clifford, the shepherd lord...... 30
Cloud-berries 37
Coniston 33, 34
Coom Scar 43
Cosh Knot 10
Cracoe 33
Craven 9, 13
Craven, three weeks tour in   12, 13
Craven Fault 10, 38, 49
Craven Archdeaconry (Parishes in).........................413
Croglin Beck 108
Cromwell Oliver, fac-simile of Autograph 40
Cross Fell 90, 106
Crosby Garrett..................... 89
Crowdundle Beck 89
Dandry Mire Viaduct............ 87
Dangerous Cave 49
Dawkins, Mr., quoted 58, 59, 70, 94
Dee, river 85, 86
Deepdale 36
Denham Wheel 76
Dew Bottom Scar 34
Dent 86, 95, 96
Dent dale......... 10, 73, 82, 85, 86
Dent Head 88, 95
Dent Head Viaduct............... 86
Deep Gill......................... 87
Dialect of Craven................. 125
Dib Scar Glen..................... 34
Doe River 68, 72
Dobson Mr., quoted " Rambles by the Ribble" 66, 67
Douk Cave 36

Douk Gill Scar	94
Dowker Bottom and Cave	35
Draughton	23
Druids' Circle	33
Dry Gill	31
Eamont River	89
Ebbing and Flowing Well	49—51
Eden Valley	82, 97—109
Eden River	10, 11, 82, 89
Eden Hall	90
Eden Brow	90
Engineering difficulties	84—86
Engineering victories	82
Eshton Hall	19
Eshton Tarn	20
Feizor	61, 66
Flasby Fell	10, 33
Forest Becks	78
Fountains Fell	10
Garsdale	82—86
Gargrave	19, 55
Gate Kirk Cave	72
Gaping Ghyll	63
Gearstones	95
Geology of Craven	110
Ghaistrill Force and Strid	33
Gill Beck	31
Giggleswick	48—51
Giggleswick School	48, 49
Giggleswick Scar	10, 34, 49
Gisburne	74, 75
Gledstone Hall	74
Gordale, Little	42, 43
Gordale Scar	31, 41, 42, 52
Grassington	33
Gray quoted	44
Greenfield Beck	37
Greenhow Hill	32
Greta river	68, 69
Graygarth	72
Hard Flask	10
Hardrow Force	96
Harker Mr., quoted	37
Hawkswick	35
Hawes	69, 87, 96
Halton Gill	35
Halton Place	78
Hanlith	39
Hebden	32
Hellifield	52
Helln Pot, Awful Chasm	94, 95
Henry VI	77
High Side	45
Hodder river	78
Horse's Head	35
Horton	60, 84, 93
Howson Mr, quoted	29, 93, 110, 125
Howgill Fells	96
Hubberholme	35, 36
Hurtle Pot	70, 71
Hartley Thos., quoted	41
Ingleton	55, 68
Ilkley	12, 21
Ingleborough	10, 65, 66, 81, 85
Ingleborough Cave	62—65
Inns	12
Jackson Mr., discovery of Victoria Cave	55—57
Janet's Cave	43
Jackdaw Hole	95
Jingle Pot	70, 71
Keighley	11
Kettlewell	34, 36
Kettlewell dale	36
Kilnsey	34
Kilnsey Scar or Crag	10, 34
Kingsdale	68, 72
Kirkby Malham	39
Kirkby Stephen	84, 87, 97, 102
Kirkoswald Castle & Church	90, 106
Lambert family	39
Langcliffe	52, 60, 82
Langcliffe Hall	52
Langstrothdale	36
Lawkland	61
Lammerside Castle	99, 101
Lazonby	90, 97, 106
Linton	32
Litton	35
Litton dale	10, 35
Long Marton	89
Long Meg and her daugters, Druidical remains	90, 109
Longwathby	90
Long Preston	52, 74, 78
Lune River	11
Lynn Gill	95
Malham	38, 44
Malham Cove	10, 34, 38, 40, 41
Malham Tarn	41, 43
Marton, East and West	74
Mallerstang Edge	87, 98
Micklefell	65, 81
Midland Railway	11
Mitton and Church	78
Moorcock Inn	87
Moughton Fell	35, 82
Mountains	10

Nappa	78	Sedbergh	87, 96
Nateby	101	Simon's Seat	10, 24, 29, 31, 32
Newbiggin	89	Skirfare, the	35
Newby Head	95	Skipton	11, 14—20
Norber	62	Skipton Castle	15—18
Normanton Dining Room	79, 80	Skyreholme	31
Norton Tower	33	Slaidburn	78
Nunnery Walks near Kirkoswald	106, 108	Smardale Viaduct	88
		Stackhouse	51, 60, 82
Ormside	89	Starbottom	36
Otley	20, 21	Stainforth	35, 51, 60
Outershaw and Beck	37	Stainforth Foss	51
Outhgill	99	Staircase Cave	49
Paley, Archdeacon	47, 48	Strid, the, Bolton Woods	24, 28
Parishes in Craven	13	Staffold Manor House	107
Paythorne	78	Stenkreth or Stankthred	101
Pendle Hill	16, 45, 55, 81	Stump Cross Caverns	31
Pendragon Castle	88, 99, 100	Sugar loaf	54
Pennine Chain	9, 81	Thirl Pot	94
Pennine Fault	87	Thornton Foss	72
Pennegent	81, 93	Thornton Beck	68
Phillips quoted	34, 65, 66, 110	Thorns Gill	95
Pudsay's Leap	77	Thorpe	32
Pudsay, Sir Ralph	78	Thund Pot	94
Pullman Car	79	Tiddeman Mr. quoted	59
Rainfall	88	Threshfield	33
Railway, Settle and Carlisle	79	Trollers Gill	31
Railway communication	11, 12	Trumla Ha'	34
Rainsber Scar	77	List of Mid. Railway Tunnels	92
Raisgill	35, 36	Upper Ribblesdale	93—95
Raisegill Hag	10	Uther Pendragon	100
Rathmell	78	Viaducts, List of, Mid. Railway	91
Ravenwray	72	Victoria Caves	35, 55—59
Ribblehead	68, 85, 95	Waddington Hall	77, 78
Ribblesdale	10, 11, 34, 82, 83	Warrendale Knots	55, 60
Ribblesdale the lower	74—78	Wensleydale	10, 96
Rimington	77	Winskill	60
Rumbold's Moor	10, 14, 21	Weathercote Cave	70, 71, 73
Rise Hill Tunnel	86	Wenning River	10, 11
Robin Hood's Mill	51	Wharfe Gill	62
Rye Loaf or Rye-loaf	10, 32, 54	Wharfe, hamlet	61
Rylstone	33	Wharfedale	21—37
Rylstone Fell	33	Wharfedale, upper	31—37
Sawley Abbey	76	Wharton Hall	88, 97, 99
Scaleber Force	45, 54	Whitaker quoted	23, 75
Scars	10	Whernside in Wharfedale	36
Scotsthrop	38	Whernside	10, 71, 73, 81, 85
Scoska Moor	10	Wigglesworth	52, 78
Sel Gill	95	Williams Mr. quoted	84, 85
Settle	11, 45, 46	Wild Boar Fell	87, 100
Settle Station	82	Yockenthwaite	36
Selside	84	Yordas Cave	72, 73

CHAPTER I.

DESCRIPTION OF THE DISTRICT AND ITS RAILWAY COMMUNICATION.

THERE are two ways of describing and defining a locality:—its artificial boundaries may be mentioned, and its several artificial divisions may be enumerated; or, its position may be brought before the mind's eye, and its characteristic features may be outlined, after the manner of physical geography, by a statement as to its mountains, its valleys and its rivers.

To proceed upon the former—the conventional method. Craven is properly an ecclesiastical appellation; it is the name of a Deanery, including 27 parishes, several of which include subordinate "districts," in the north-west of Yorkshire. The term is, however, somewhat loosely and popularly applied, and is considered to include nearly the whole of the Wapontake of Staincliffe and a part of Ewcross, with smaller portions of Skirack and Claro.

On the south and west the boundary of Craven extends to the County Palatine of Lancaster. It will, however, be more interesting to the reader to be informed of the situation and the distinctive features of the region about to be described in detail.

The range of mountains which runs north and south, from the borders of Scotland into Derbyshire, is known as the Penine Chain. It forms the watershed of the north of England: the rivers rising on its slopes finding their way either eastward into the German Ocean, or westward into the Irish Sea. A glance at the map will show that there are two rivers, the Aire and the Wharfe, which, rising in the highlands of Yorkshire, flow into the Ouse, and so into the Humber; and that there is a river, the Ribble, which flows into the sea below Preston, in Lancashire.

The district, to which this book proposes to be a guide, includes the sources and the earlier portions of the courses of these three rivers. There are tributaries to all three, and there are other rivers, such as the Wenning, which do not flow into any of them. But the above is a definition accurate enough.

But this is offered as a Guide, not only to Craven, but to the Settle and Carlisle Railway. Now, that line touches the head both of Dentdale and of Wensleydale, but the greater portion of it, after Ribblesdale has been penetrated to the river's source, follows the course of the Eden, from its rise nearly to its outflow into the sea, below Carlisle.

Wharfedale, Airedale, and Ribblesdale; these are the three great valleys of Craven. Now, these valleys thread their way amidst mountains which are among the most lofty in England, being only exceeded in elevation by the peaks to the westward, in the neighbourhood of the Lakes. Ingleborough and Whernside on the west, and Pennygent on the east of Ribblesdale; Rye Loaf and Hard Flask in the vicinity of the source of the Aire, and Flasby Fell and Rumbold's Moor among the heights that overlook the course of the same river; Great and Little Whernside, and Buckden and Ramsden's Pikes on the eastern side of the Wharfe; Buckden Birks, Horse Head, and Raisegill Hag, between Littondale and the Upper Wharfedale; Simon Seat and Barden Fell lower down Wharfedale; and in a central line through the district, south and north, Fountains Fell, Scoska Moor, Cosh Knot and Cam Fell;—these may be taken as the more prominent and noticeable of these Craven fells and mountains.

There is a feature of the hill scenery of this district which calls for special attention. The traveller will observe in several parts of Craven 'scars' or cliffs of a very remarkable character. These are precipitous bare escarpments of limestone rock. The most interesting of these are Kilnsey Crag, Malham Cove, Attermire Rocks, and Giggleswick Scar. Several of these scars mark the lines of the great Craven fault,—a displacement of the limestone formation, which has left most unmistakeable traces upon the face of the country, and which is the cause of not a little of the picturesque scenery of Craven.

The geological character of the district is extremely interesting, and will be found described in another chapter. The observant traveller will not fail to note the signs of the geological formation unmistakeably evident in the general aspect of the country, and in the prevalent vegetation. He will remark the slates of Ribblesdale, the limestone rocks which are the feature of Craven, the capping of millstone grit upon the summits of several of the loftiest mountains, and the conglomerate sandstone which forms the lovely valley of the Eden.

So distinguishing a characteristic is the mountainous and craggy nature of this region that it is embedded in the very name by which it is designated. Craven is believed to be Craig Vaen, "the stony rock," and appears equivalent in meaning to Staincliffe, the name of the Wapontake which is largely coincident with the ecclesiastical division,—the Deanery.

The prevailing character of Craven is pastoral. At Bingley, Keighley, and Skipton, there are considerable manufactures, and here and there in the valleys the tourist will come upon a cotton mill, giving employment to the population. But agriculture is the chief occupation of the inhabitants of Craven; and the land is chiefly pasture and meadow land, the amount of arable soil being very small. Indeed, in the higher valleys there is often not a single ploughed field to be seen, look where you will. Cattle and sheep are reared, fed, and fattened in abundance. Especially since the great rise in the price of meat, it is this department of farming which has been found most profitable by the "statesmen" and the "dalesmen," of the north-west of England.

The country bordering the Settle and Carlisle Railway is, for the first half of the way, altogether pastoral; but in the valley of the Eden, from Appleby downwards, corn is grown in considerable quantity, and the ordinary green crops appear to flourish

The district to which this book professes to be a guide is easily accessible by railway from every part of England. The Midland Railway runs right through the heart of Craven, from Bingley, by Keighley and Skipton to Settle, and thence pursues its way to Carlisle, as described in Chapters x., xi., and xii. The traveller from London or the midland counties will, of necessity take this route, via Normanton and Leeds: and the tourist approaching from Scotland will be careful to leave Carlisle by the 'new route.' From Lancaster and its neighbourhood, the approach to Craven is also by the Midland line, up the valleys of the Lune and the Wenning.

The tourist from Liverpool, Manchester, and most other parts of Lancashire, will find the Lancashire and Yorkshire route by Colne the most convenient for reaching Skipton.

Should the visitor to Craven desire, in the first instance, to explore Wharfedale, commencing at Ilkley, he can reach Ilkley from Leeds by the Midland or by the North Eastern Railway, or from Harrogate by the latter.

Once in the district the tourist will find no difficulty in reaching any place described in this Guide. The pedestrian will often be able to avail himself of the help of the Midland Railway in passing over the less inviting portions of his route. There is an omnibus which conveys the mails daily from Skipton to Wharfedale. Carriages, dog-carts, and waggonettes may be hired at all the towns and some of the villages of Craven; and saddle horses and ponies may be procured at many of the village inns, and will be found very suitable for mountain excursions.

As for the inns, the tourist may confidently reckon upon cleanliness and good fare, as well as attentive treatment. If he visit the remoter valleys, he must expect humble entertainment. Mountain mutton, trout from the becks, cream from the dairy, heath honey from the hives, are specialities of the district; and he must be hard to please who does not acknowledge, at the close of a tour in Craven, that he has fared well.

A THREE WEEKS' TOUR IN CRAVEN AND THE SETTLE AND CARLISLE DISTRICT:—

Monday......Skipton: Church and Castle.
Tuesday......Bolton, Ilkley, and Ben Rhydding.
Wednesday...Barden Tower and Simon's Seat; Grassington.
Thursday ...Wharfedale: Kilnsey, Dowkerbottom, Kettlewell
Friday........Wharfedale, Littondale, and Langstrothdale.
Saturday ....Bolton Priory and Woods.
Sunday.......Rest at Bolton.
Monday......Malham and Gordale, *via* Skipton and Bell Busk.
Tuesday .....Settle: Giggleswick Scar, School, and Well.
Wednesday...Attermire, Scaleber, and Victoria Cave.
Thursday ...Horton, climb Pennegent, Helln Pot.
Friday........Austwick, Clapham, the Cave.
Saturday ....Climb Ingleborough, or a long excursion into
                Lower Ribblesdale.
Sunday.......Rest at Clapham
Monday......Ingleton, Thornton, Chapel-le-dale, Weathercote, Gearstones.

Tuesday......Ribblehead, Thorns Gill, Blea Moor.
Wednesday ..Dentdale.
Thursday ...Hawes and Upper Wensleydale.
Friday........Kirkby Stephen, Wharton Hall, Pendragon Castle.
Saturday ....Appleby, Long Meg, Lazonby, and Nunnery Walks.
Sunday......Rest at Carlisle.

NOTE TO CHAPTER I.

The following are the parishes included in the Archdeaconry of Craven,—which is one of the two Archdeaconries of the Diocese of Ripon, that of Richmond being the other :

Northern Division.	*Western Division.*	*Southern Division.*
Arncliffe	Barnoldswick	Addingham
Halton Gill	Bolton-by-Bowland	Bingley
Hubberholme	Bracewell	Holy Trinity
Burnsall, with	Broughton	Cullingworth
Rylstone and	Carlton	Moughton
Conistone	Lothersdale	Morton with
Gargrave	Gisburne	Morton Banks
Conistone	Tosside	Bolton Abbey
Giggleswick	Marton	Ilkley
Langcliffe	Mitton	Keighley
Rathmell	Grindleton	Eastwood
Settle	Hurst Green	Oakworth
Stainforth	Waddington	Ingrow cum-Hainworth
Horton-in-Ribblesdale	Skipton	
Kettlewell	Christchurch	Kildwick
Kirkby Malhamdale	Embsay	Cononley
Linton	Slaidburn with	Cowling
Long Preston	Dale Head	Silsden
	Thornton-in-Craven	Sutton
	Kellbrooke	

CHAPTER II.

SKIPTON.

Inns:— Devonshire Arms and Black Horse.

UNDER the south-western slope of Rumbold's Moor, in the valley af the Aire and on its left bank, at a distance of 26 miles from Leeds and 18 from Bradford —is Skipton, the capital of Craven. The name (from A. S. scep,—sheep) points to the pastoral nature of the district, which is and has long been famous for cattle and sheep. There is a fortnightly cattle market, also cattle and horse fairs of some importance. The population in 1871 was 9,505, and the number of houses 1946.

Approaching the town from the new and commodious station of the Midland Railway, the visitor crosses the Leeds and Liverpool Canal, and enters the main street, which is broad and would be decidedly handsome but for the "middle row," or block of houses in the midst of its lower portion. The houses are built of stone, and in the street are some good modern buildings, shops, banking-houses, &c. In the suburbs are some very neat modern villas. There are several cotton factories, giving employment to a large number of hands. The quarrying of the limestone for building is one of the great industries of Skipton.

There is a well-endowed Grammar School, formerly free, but now, under a new scheme, open to all upon payment of moderate school fees. The new school buildings are handsome and commodious

The Craven Baths and Pump Room have been erected for the utilization of the saline sulphuretted spring; they will be found at the eastern part of the town.

There are two churches, and places of worship for Wesleyans, Independents, &c. The modern church, Christ church, is in the direction of the railway station.

At the head of the chief street, and in proximity to one another, are the two "lions" of Skipton—the Castle and the Church.

The Castle of Skipton is chiefly associated with the historical family of the Cliffords. Skipton, which was before the Conquest the property of Earl Edwin, was granted by William the Conqueror to Robert de Romillé, who is believed to have built the original castle. It passed by descent to the family of Albemarle, but in the reign of Edward I. came into possession of the Crown. Edward II. bestowed Skipton upon his favourite, Piers de Gaveston; and afterwards on Robert de Clifford, who had fought under Edward I. against the Scotch, and who afterwards fell at Bannockburn, in 1314. Except that an attainder occurred in the first year of Edward IV. to Lord John Clifford, who had sided with the Lancastrian party, and who was killed the day before the battle of Towton, Skipton remained in the possession of the Cliffords for upwards of three centuries, and indeed, has remained in the hands of their descendents to the present time.

The best known and most famous of the family have been—the eighth lord, who fell at the battle of St. Albans; his son, the "black-faced Clifford," who fell at Ferrybridge; and his son, known as the "shepherd lord," because, during the attainder above referred to, he was hidden, by his mother's care, among the shepherds of Cumberland for 24 years. The next lord was created Earl of Cumberland by Henry VIII., and it was by him that the more modern portion of the Castle was built. The famous Lady Anne Clifford was the daughter of the third Earl, and was successively Countess of Dorset and of Pembroke. She was born in Skipton Castle, January, 1590, and lived until 1675, when she died at Appleby, where she lies buried. She restored this and others of her castles; Skipton the more needing it as it had endured a three years' siege by the Parliamentarian troops during the Civil War.

From Lady Anne Clifford Skipton came to the Earls of Thanet, her grandsons, whose descendant, Sir Henry Tufton, is its present owner.

As we approach the Castle we feel how completely it must have dominated the little town below. There are at the entrance two round towers with the gateway between them. Over the gateway is a coat of arms, and above this, in large letters of stone, forming a kind of parapet and standing out in singular relief against the sky, the word DESORMAIS.—

the family motto of the Cliffords. We ring and are admitted, and, after glancing at a grotesque room in the gateway, stuck all round with shells, and remarking the groove for the ancient portcullis on the inner side of the archway, proceed, under the guidance of the janitor, to survey the buildings. On the right is a modern residence inhabited by servants, who keep it in order for the occasional use of the steward. The apartments here contain some interesting tapestry, said to date from the time of Henry IV., and some family portraits.

We ascend a flight of stairs on the left, and enter the old Castle buildings. Over the door is a shield engraven with amorial quarterings, and an inscription from which we learn that the Castle was restored in 1657—58, by that great "restorer of waste places," Lady Anne Clifford. The stairs lead up to the Inner Court, which we found cool and shady on a hot day of August. In the middle is a fine yew tree, estimated to be from 500 to 700 years old, which divides into three branches, and almost fills the court with its lofty and spreading growth; a stone seat surrounds the trunk. Here is an ancient octagonal font, which was removed from the private chapel of the Cliffords. Over one doorway in this court we observe the stone effigy of the Griffin—the Clifford crest; over another the arms of Piers de Gaveston, the favourite of Edward II.

The apartments of the Castle are in an uninhabitable and anything but attractive condition, but they are of great interest, as shewing the arrangements of a fortified building of the period. There are no two rooms upon the same level, and there is not one room in the Castle which has not two doors,—it is said, in order to facilitate escape in case of surprise. We were led through a gloomy store-room into a circular guard-room, the walls of which we remarked as being ten feet in thickness; and thence into a bedroom, which, tradition tells, was the birth-place of Fair Rosamund, whose reputed inner chamber adjoins it. Ascending the staircase and passing sundry bedrooms, we reached the leaded roof of the watch-tower. Hence we enjoyed a fine view: looking south, we saw Skipton streets, mills, and churches below us, and the valley of the Aire, with Carleton Moors beyond; looking east, the landscape was soon bounded by the massive heights of Rumbold's Moor; northwards, Embsay Moor stretched before us; whilst the prospect on the west was bounded by the ubiquitous outlines of Pendle Hill. Just below and beyond the Castle, northwards, the landscape is enriched by the pretty Skipton Woods, consisting of beech, ash, fir, and bastard sycamores. Every room, as we descend from the leads, has a separate roof of its own, and there is a promenade among the roofs all over the Castle.

Returning, we passed through the best bedroom, which had formerly a carved oak ceiling, until, after the surrender of the Castle, all the carved oak was burned, of course by Oliver Cromwell! We observed that, as usual, all the outer windows are merely loop-holes; all the windows admitting any amount of light open to the inner court. Fancy easily re-constructs these old apartments, with their windows not of glass, but horn, their floors covered not with carpets, but with rushes, their walls hung with tapestry, and their open fire-places with blazing logs upon the dog-irons!

From a dimly lighted drawing-room a door leads to the muniment room, where the deeds and papers relating to the estate are said still to be kept. Dark passages led us to the circular room which tradition has denominated Mary's room, and which, it is fabled, Mary, Queen of Scots occupied as a resting place, when on her way southwards in the custody of a Clifford. From the window of the morning or breakfast room we looked out and remarked water gleaming here and there amongst dense foliage. Just under the Castle walls is a branch of the Leeds and Liverpool Canal; beyond is a small culvert; and beyond that, part of the old moat, now converted into a mill dam. The ancient banqueting-hall, which is low and by no means imposing, is still used upon the occasions when the tenants of Sir Henry Tufton dine in the Castle under the presidency of the steward. A landing, passing the buttery hatch, led us to the kitchen, which seemed to us the most interesting apartment in the Castle. There are two grand kitchen fire-places, one at each end of the apartment; and as we looked up the great chimneys to the sky, we fancied how, in the old days of rude hospitality, the log fires must have roared when the preparations were going forward for some lordly feast! Passing the steward's pantry and bedroom, we descended by a flight of steps to the dungeon, a damp, musty-smelling prison, some sixteen feet by seven, with the solid rock for its floor, and at the entrance, the still remaining apertures for bolts of frightful security.

The bulk of the old Castle is Edwardian, though there is a Norman doorway partially concealed by the present entrance.

Some of the upper portions of the walls are said to be the work of Lady Anne Clifford, who restored the building; they are not so massive, which tradition accounts for by saying that her ladyship was not allowed to repair the place as a stronghold.

Part of the outer wall towards the town still remains; it is seven feet in thickness. The site of the moat is now occupied by the high road, running without and below the wall.

Close by the Castle is the Church, the tower of which was, it is said, battered by the Parliamentary forces during the siege already alluded to: the damage was, however, made good by the redoubtable Countess, in 1655.

The Church is approached by a new porch, the gift of Mr. Robinson, in 1850; itself handsome enough, but in the decorated Gothic style, and scarcely in keeping with the Perpendicular building. In the south aisle are four sedilia of the 13th century, of admirable design. The whole building was repaired in 1665—of course, by Lady Anne Clifford—and after being struck by lightning, was again partially restored in 1853. A flight of seven steps leads up to the altar. The handsome reredos, of Caen Stone, costing £800, was erected in 1874, as a memorial of Mr. Henry Alcock by eight of his children. The handsome screen has been recently restored. In 1876 a new organ was provided at a cost of £700.

Observe the stained glass windows, four of which are Belgian, by Capronnier, of Brussels. The subject of one is St. Luke, a memorial to a physician,—Dr. Marsden. Another is in memory of Mr. Birtwhistle; the subjects are, "The Bearing of the Cross." "The Agony," and "The Appearance to Mary." There are also windows by Cox, of London.

The oaken roof is flat, and is very beautifully carved; it is probably of the 16th century.

Above the west gallery, upon the wall, is a singular work of art. It is a picture, not painted, but burnt into panels of sycamore wood, no colour at all having been used, and the whole effect, which is by no means contemptible, being produced by burning. It is said that a hot poker was the instrument employed! The artist was a native of Skipton, named Smith. The subject appears to be "The Vision of Angels by the Shepherds."

But the most interesting feature in Skipton Church is its monuments. There is an ancient altar slab in the north chancel, in which also should be remarked the stones marking the vaults where lie interred the former head-masters of the grammar-school of the town.

A stone tablet upon the wall bears the following very touching inscription: "IMMENSI DOLORIS MONUMENTUM ANGUSTUM. HENRICUS PATER DEFLET FRANCISCUM, CHAROLUM, HENRICUM, A.D. MDXXXI."

In the chancel are three monumental tombs of the Cliffords, all of which have been recently restored, under the superintendence of Sir Gilbert Scott, and at the expense of the present Duke of Devonshire. Several brasses belonging to these tombs were found at a farm-house in the neighbourhood, and were restored to their proper position; and new brasses, to match the old, have been inserted in the vacant spaces. One large tomb, that on the north side, is to the memory of Sir Henry Clifford, who became first Earl of Cumberland, and Margaret, his wife, a daughter of Sir Henry Percy, of Northumberland. At the head of this tomb is a brass commemorative of three generations. The effigies are all in brass; the head-stone contains an emblematical representation of the Trinity.

On the south side of the chancel is a tomb of black marble, that of the third Earl of Cumberland, and father of the famous Lady Anne. This monument is remarkable for the heraldic adornments it displays. Here are 17 shields of armorial bearings; six on each side, two at the feet, and three at the head!

Nine of the Clifford family lie in vaults under the chancel of this Church. All, excepting one, are enclosed in leads fitting the figure of the body.

Near the tower, is a Library, bequeathed in 1719 by Silvester Petyt, whose portrait hangs in the vestry. There are some ancient books; we noticed a history of the world, printed in the year 1497.

GARGRAVE is the next station to Skipton. The village is situated among verdant meadows. Tradition tells that there were once seven churches in Gargrave, but that six were destroyed by the Scots in one of their excursions, the one remaining church being spared because dedicated to St. Andrew, the patron saint of Scotland.

Half-a-mile from the village was discovered the site of a Roman villa, but no traces of it are now to be seen.

A mile and a half from Gargrave is the seat of Sir Matthew Wilson, M.P., Eshton Hall, a spacious mansion in which is a fine library of 15,000 volumes, said to be peculiarly rich in the natural sciences, topography, and history. There are also valuable manuscripts and some fine paintings.

Above the Hall is St. Helen's Well, a copious opening from which a streamlet flows which waters the park.

Eshton Tarn is a small lake less than two miles in circumference. Since the draining of Giggleswick Tarn, Malham and Eshton remain the only lakes in Craven.

Distances from Skipton:—To Ilkley, 9 miles; to Bolton Bridge, 6 miles; to Barden, 6 miles; to Grassington, 11 miles; to Malham, 11 miles.

CHAPTER III.

WHARFEDALE.

IT will be convenient to the reader that this chapter should be divided into three sections, treating respectively of Ilkley, of Bolton and Barden, and of the Upper Wharfe. The Wharfe, it may be premised, is the Verbeia of the Romans, and the Guerf of the Saxons.

I.—ILKLEY.

Inns :—Crescent Hotel, Lister's Arms, and Rose and Crown.

Although the pedestrian may approach Ilkley from Leeds by way of Otley Chevin, Otley, and Burley, and—as we have done more than once in younger days—may even walk from Leeds in the early summer morning and reach Ilkley in time for breakfast, yet, we will suppose the visitor to arrive by train, and to begin his explorations of Wharfedale at this modern and beautifully situated watering-place.

With the swift flowing Wharfe in the valley below, bordered by its bright meadows,—with the timbered park of Middleton Hall on the northern slope opposite—with the heights of Rumbold's Moor behind, rising to an elevation of over 1,300 feet—with its snug hotels and well-placed "water establishments,"—Ilkley may well boast of its charming situation. A few years ago, and it was a quiet village, with an old-fashioned inn, and some primitive lodging houses, and above all, the Cold Bath, in the little stone hut on the hill side. Now, there are hotels and "establishments," handsome new churches and elegant villas; and Ilkley aspires to be "the Malvern of the north." However, the valley is as lovely as ever, and the moors as breezy and exhilarating; and parties of young people may still be met with crossing the Wharfe upon the old stepping stones, or clambering to the top of the Cow and Calf rocks, or gathering bilberries on the moor, as of old.

Ben Rhydding is a large and imposing looking building, in the Scottish Baronial style, devoted to the accommodation of patients under the "cold water treatment." It was opened in 1844, but has been since enlarged. There is a Turkish bath, a compressed air bath, and indeed baths of every description. Plenty of amusements are provided:—billiard rooms, a bowling green, a bowling alley, croquet lawns, and a racket court, are well adapted to "drive away dull care." There are extensive grounds attached to the house, and better still, the heathery moors immediately adjoin the estate.

This well-known and largely frequented establishment is situated above a mile to the east of Ilkley; but it has a railway station of its own for the use of the inmates.

Ilkley Wells House was built some years subsequently, in 1856. It stands in the higher part of Ilkley, and like Ben Rhydding, commands fine views over the valley of the Wharfe. This mansion is in the Italian style, and contains every convenience and luxury.

Boarders not in need of hydropathic treatment are received at both these establishments.

There are also houses where patients of a poorer class can enjoy the benefit of the water cure.

Ilkley was a Roman station, and had, before the occupation by the Romans, been one of the cities of the Brigantes; it is called by Ptolemy, "Olicana." Some foundations of the Roman fortress may yet be traced, and Roman remains are not infrequently found in the vicinity.

The Church has been recently restored and partially re-built. It is in the early Decorated style. The most interesting relic of antiquity is a cross-legged effigy in the south aisle, usually considered to be that of Sir Adam de Middleton.

In the church-yard are three very ancient sculptured crosses, concerning which much has been conjectured, but little determined. They are delineated in lithograph in Professor Phillip's well-known book on Yorkshire.

II.—BOLTON AND BARDEN.

Inns:—Devonshire Arms and Red Lion.

The drive or walk of six miles from Ilkley to Bolton is extremely beautiful. The road follows the course of the

Wharfe on its right or western bank, and passes through the village of Addingham, where is the junction with the carriage-road from Skipton to Ilkley.

The visitor to Bolton who comes from Skipton in Airedale will not, however, travel as far south as Addingham. He must pass through Draughton; the distance is only six miles.

Bolton, with its Abbey and its woods, is justly acknowledged to be one of the most beautiful spots in our beautiful island. Whitaker, who was an enthusiastic admirer of this portion of Wharfedale especially, has characterized the landscape in words which have often been quoted, but which the reader will be glad to have before him in this place :- - .

"Bolton Priory stands upon a beautiful curvature of the Wharfe, on a level sufficiently elevated to protect it from inundation, and low enough for every purpose of picturesque effect. In the latter respect it has no equal among the northern houses, perhaps not in the kingdom. Fountains, as a building, is more entire, more spacious and magnificent, but the valley of the Skell is insignificant and without features. Furness, which is more dilapidated, ranks still lower in point of situation. Kirkstall, as a mere ruin, is superior to Bolton, but though deficient neither in wood nor water, it wants the seclusion of the deep valley, and the termination of a bold, rocky background. Tintern, which perhaps most resembles it, has rock, wood, and water in perfection, but no foreground whatever. Opposite to the magnificent east window of the Priory Church, the river washes a rock, nearly perpendicular, and of the richest purple, where several of the mineral beds instead of maintaining their usual inclination to the horizon, are twisted, by some inconceivable process, into undulating and spiral lines. To the south all is soft and delicious; the eye reposes on a few rich pastures and a moderate reach of the river, sufficiently tranquil to form a mirror to the sun, and to the bounding fells beyond, neither too near nor too lofty to exclude, even in winter, any portion of his rays. But after all, the glories of Bolton are on the north. Whatever the most fastidious taste could require to constitute a landscape, is not only found here, but in its proper place. In front, and immediately under the eye, is a smooth expanse of park-like enclosure, spotted with native elm, ash, &c., of the finest growth; on the right, a skirting oak wood, with jutting points of grey rock; on the left a rising copse. Still forward are seen the aged groves of Bolton Park, the growth of centuries;

and farther yet, the barren and rocky distances of Simon's Seat and Barden Fell, contrasted to the warmth, fertility, and luxuriant foliage of the valley below."

Bolton Priory is a foundation dating from the twelfth century. A monastery for Augustinian Canons was founded at Embsay, in 1120, by William de Meschines and his wife, Cecilia de Romillé. After a lapse of 33 years "the canons were removed to Bolton by William Fitz Duncan and his wife, another Cecilia de Romillé, the only child and heiress of the founders of the house at Embsay." It was their son who was known as the "boy of Egremond," who was, according to tradition, drowned in the Strid, and whose death is said to have been the occasion of the erection of the Priory at Bolton.

One of the chief points of interest at Bolton is the Strid, two miles higher up the river, where the Wharfe is contracted within ledges of rock, between which, especially when swollen by rain, the river rushes with a deep and solemn roar, like the voice of the angry spirit of the waters, heard far above and beneath, amidst the silence of the surrounding woods. The channel at this spot is little more than four feet across, and is often leaped by the adventurous. Indeed, the word "Strid" has usually been regarded as the same as "stride," from the possibility of striding the river at this point. But the true derivation is probably from the Anglo-Saxon "Stryth," which means turmoil, tumult.

This is the scene of the tragic incident which has been versified in the well-known poem of Wordsworth, "The Force of Prayer." We subjoin this poem, as not only giving a romantic interest to Bolton Strid, but as embodying the popular tradition as to the foundation of Bolton Priory. It should be added that there is evidence that "the boy of Egremond" lived to be a man; but the tradition may have an authentic origin in the fate of some other member of the family.

"What is good for a bootless bene?"
   With these dark words begins my tale ;
And their meaning is, whence can comfort spring
   When prayer is of no avail ?

"What is good for a bootless bene?"
   The Falconer to the Lady said ;
And she made answer, "endless sorrow,"
   For she knew that her son was dead,

She knew it by the Falconer's words,
　　And from the look of the Falconer's eye;
And from the love which was in her soul,
　　For her youthful Romilly.

—Young Romilly through Barden woods
　　Is ranging high and low,
And holds a greyhound in his leash,
　　To let slip upon buck or doe.

The pair have reached that fearful chasm,
　　How tempting to bestride!
For lordly Wharfe is there pent in
　　With rocks on either side.

This striding place is called THE STRID,
　　A name which it took of yore;
A thousand years hath it borne that name,
　　And shall a thousand more.

And hither is young Romilly come,
　　And what may now forbid
That he, perhaps for the hundredth time,
　　Shall bound across the Strid?

He sprang in glee,—for what cared he
　　That the river was strong, and the rocks were steep?—
But the greyhound in the leash hung back,
　　And checked him in his leap

The boy is in the arms of Wharfe,
　　And strangled by a merciless force;
For never more was young Romilly seen
　　Till he rose a lifeless corse.

Now there is stillness in the vale,
　　And long, unspeaking sorrow:
Wharfe shall be to pitying eyes,
　　A name more sad than Yarrow.

If for a lover the Lady wept,
　　A solace she might borrow;
From death, and from the passion of death;
　　Old Wharfe might heal her sorrow

She weeps not for the wedding-day,
　　Which was to be to-morrow;
Her hope was a further-looking hope,
　　And hers is a mother's sorrow.

He was a tree that stood alone,
　　And proudly did its branches wave,
And the root of this delightful tree
　　Was in her husband's grave.

C

> Long, long in darkness did she sit,
>   And her first words were, "Let there be
> In Bolton, on the field of Wharfe,
>   A stately Priory!"
>
> The stately Priory was reared,
>   And Wharfe, as he moved along,
> To matins joined a mournful voice,
>   Nor failed at even-song.
>
> And the Lady prayed in heaviness
>   That looked not for relief!
> But slowly did her succour come,
>   And a patience to her grief.
>
> Oh! there is never sorrow of heart
>   That shall lack a timely end,
> If but to God we turn, and ask
>   Of Him to be our Friend!

The foundation of Bolton was liberally endowed, and the establishment, consisting of more than 200 persons, was well provided for. Those who are curious in such matters should read in *Whitaker's History of Craven* the specimens printed there from the old account books. Although Landseer's well-known picture, "Bolton Abbey in the Olden Time," contains nothing specially characteristic of this Priory, it serves to remind us how earth, air, and water, were all laid under contribution for the supply of the wants of the saintly brethren, whilst they were still in the fleshly tabernacle, and abiding in the wilderness of earth.

Bolton Hall, a house of the Duke of Devonshire, is modern, except the central part, which was the ancient gateway of the Abbey.

Of the Priory, only the church remains. The nave, partly Early English and partly Decorated, has been restored and is used as a parish church. The lancet windows on the south have been filled with modern stained glass. Below the chantry chapel is the vault of the Claphams of Beamsley and the Mauleverers.

> "Pass, pass who will, yon chantry door;
> And, through the chink in the fractured floor,
> Look down, and see a griesly sight;
> A vault where the bodies are buried upright!
> There, face by face, and hand by hand,
> The Claphams and Mauleverers stand;
> And, in his place, among son and sire,
> Is John de Clapham, that fierce Esquire,

> A valiant man, and a name of dread
> In the ruthless wars of the White and Red ;
> Who dragged Earl Pembroke from Banbury Church,
> And smote off his head on the stones of the porch!
> Oft does the White Doe loiter there,
> Prying into the darksome rent."

The transepts and the choir are chiefly of the Decorated period, and some of the tracery remains and is very beautiful, although much is gone. At the east end is some arcading in the transition Norman style, very elegant.

A western tower in the Perpendicular style was commenced in 1520 by Prior Moon, but was never finished. It is thought probable that there was a central tower; but no tower now remains, and the want of one is the chief defect of Bolton in the matter of picturesqueness, as compared with Kirkstall or Fountains.

There are some traces of the cloister-court and of the chapter-house. The present rectory is on the site of the monastery kitchens.

The church-yard is on the north side of the Priory. It was hither, according to the tradition and the poem, that the survivor of the Nortons, Emily, attended by her White Doe, was wont to repair.

> "But most to Bolton's sacred pile,
> On favouring nights she loved to go;
> There ranged through cloister, court, and aisle,
> Attended by the soft-paced Doe;
> Nor feared she in the still moonshine
> To look upon St. Mary's shrine;
> Nor on the lowly turf that showed
> Where Francis slept in his last abode.
> There oft she came, there oft she sate,
> Forlorn, but not disconsolate;
> And, when she from the abyss returned
> Of thought, she neither shrunk nor mourned;
> Was happy that she lived to greet
> Her mute companion as it lay
> In love and pity at her feet."

And it was hither that, after Emily's death, the Doe is represented as having frequented her mistress's grave.

> "Haunting the spots with lonely cheer,
> Which her dear mistress once held dear;
> Loves most what Emily loved most—
> The enclosure of this church-yard ground;

Here wanders, like a gliding ghost,
And every Sabbath here is found.

* * * *

But chiefly by that single grave,
That one sequestered hillock green,
The pensive visitant is seen."

Bolton Woods contain some of the most delightful scenery in all England. The visitor will do well to linger here; it is not the place for a hurried visit, but rather for a week of rural leisure. It is worth while to reprint here Wordsworth's* judgment upon the landscapes of Bolton, penned when these scenes were less known than now :—

"I cannot conclude without recommending to the notice of all lovers of beautiful scenery Bolton Abbey and its neighbourhood. This enchanting spot belongs to the Duke of Devonshire; and the superintendence of it has for some years been entrusted to the Rev. William Carr, who has most skilfully opened out its features; and in whatever he has added has done justice to the place, by working with the invisible hand of art in the very spirit of nature."

Seats have been placed in some of the most eligible positions in these woods, each of which commands a distinct view with its own special charms. This accommodation adds much to the comfort and enjoyment of the visitor.

The two following walks may be recommended to the visitor to Bolton Abbey who is not pressed for time.

(1.) Start from the Holme Terrace and pass the Hall and the Abbey. On passing the west front of the Abbey, the road is regained. A walk of a mile will lead to a wooden bridge over the Wharfe; cross this, and a footpath to the left will take you to Lud's Cave and Lud-stream Seat. Crossing the bridge over Possforth Beck you will arrive at the Strid; from thence the visitor may proceed along the river to a point opposite the mouth of Barden Beck, where he will obtain an excellent view of Barden Tower. Hence, he may return by the Oak, Clifford, the Strid, and Boyleford Seats, up Possforth Beck to Lawn Seat, Buckrake Seat, and the Devonshire Seat, from which the cascade is distant only a few hundred yards. The Valley of Desolation extends for half-a-mile beyond the cascade. The havoc caused by a terrific thunderstorm long since has left traces which still justify the name of this valley. From the smaller cascade at the top of the Valley of

* Note to "The White Doe of Rylstone."

Desolation, the visitor may return by the east side, and across the park to Park-gate Seat, whence a very fine view may be enjoyed. The wooden bridge must then be re-crossed, and a footpath across the fields leads to the "Devonshire Arms."

(2.) The second ramble commences by crossing the bridge to the eastern side of the Wharfe. Take the first gate on the left, which leads to a seat under a large elm at the river's bank. The next seat, a circular one round an oak, is Skip-house-wheel Seat, and may be reached either by the path to the right following the beaten track through the field, or by that to the left, winding round the base of the rock, and ascending by a flight of rude steps. After passing the Waterfall Bridge, the next seats are Cat-crag, Prior's, and Prior's-stone Seats; from hence there is a bridge over Noscow Gill. But follow the footpath to the left to Burlington Seat, and the way is plain to Simon's Seat, St. Bridget's Seat, and so over the wooden bridge to Pembroke Seat. From this point the best view of Barden Tower is obtained; a rocky island divides the Wharfe into two channels, it is fringed with wood or meadow on both sides, and the forest trees are seen towering up to the very base of the ruin. Passing in succession Lady Harriet's, the Cavendish, and Lady Georgiana's Seats, you reach the finest point of view in the whole domain, —Hartington Seat. After enjoying the lovely landscape which stretches before you here, you return to the Abbey.*

The imaginative visitor, lingering among Bolton ruins and woods a summer day, will take pleasure in picturing the aspect of the famous Priory in the olden time. The lines of Wordsworth will help him to portray the scenes of bygone days:—

> "From Bolton's old monastic tower
> The bells ring loud with gladsome power;
> The sun shines bright; the fields are gay
> With people in their best array
> Of stole and doublet, hood and scarf,
> Along the banks of crystal Wharfe,
> Through the vale retired and lowly,
> Trooping to that summons holy.
> And, up among the moorlands, see
> What sprinklings of blithe company!
> Of lasses and of shepherd grooms,
> That down the steep hills force their way,
> Like cattle through the budded brooms;
> Path, or no path, what care they?

*The description of the above walks is substantially that of Mr. Howson.

> And thus in joyous mood they hie
> To Bolton's mouldering Priory."

BARDEN TOWER is chiefly interesting as having been the residence of Henry Clifford, the "shepherd lord." His family being of the Lancastrian party, this Clifford was "in hiding" among the fells of Cumberland for upwards of twenty years, during the ascendancy of the Yorkists. After the accession of Henry VII., and the reconciliation of the two factions, the Cliffords, like other proscribed families, were restored to their inheritance. The "shepherd lord" made Barden his home, and about the year 1485 converted Barden Lodge into a residence. About a century afterwards it became a ruin; but was restored by Lady Anne Clifford in the years 1658 and 1659,—as may be read in a curious and characteristic inscription still remaining over the principal doorway. Though entire, according to Dr. Whitaker, in 1774, it has for some time been again a ruin. The chapel, however, was restored by the Duke of Devonshire, in 1860; and part of the adjoining tower is used as a farm-house. The old key of the Tower and a rusty halberd are the only antiquities belonging to the place which are still preserved. The ruins are picturesque, but by no means imposing.

The visitor may well muse upon the vicissitudes of great families, as he lingers by—

> "The shy recess
> Of Barden's humble quietness."

And his reminiscences of the "good Lord Clifford" will be pleasant:—

> "As Clifford erst in Barden's neighbouring tower,
> The Shepherd Lord unscathed by civil jars,
> Undazzled by the blaze of sudden power,
> Trained his meek spirit 'mid the silent stars."

This Lord Clifford is said to have been a student of astronomy and alchemy, in which studies he was aided by the monks of Bolton. Notwithstanding his peaceful tastes and habits, he fought at Flodden Field in 1513, and led the warriors from the Craven country, who formed part of the English host.

> "From Pennegent to Pendle Hill,
> From Linton to Long Addingham,
> And all that Craven coasts could till,
> They with the lusty Clifford came;

All Staincliffe hundred went with him,
With striplings strong from Wharfedale,
And all that Halton Hills did climb,
With Lougstroth eke and Litton Dale,
Whose milk-fed fellows, fleshly bred,
Well browned, with sounding bows upbend,
All such as Horton Fells had fed,
On Clifford's banner did attend."

The "shepherd lord" died at the age of seventy, ten years after the battle of Flodden, in 1523.

Distances from Bolton:—To Ilkley, 5 miles; to Grassington, 10 miles; to Kilnsey, 14 miles; to Kettlewell, 17 miles; to Skipton, 6 miles; to Harrogate, 16 miles.

III.—UPPER WHARFEDALE.

From Barden Bridge a *détour* should be made to Gill Beck, which, tracking a ravine rich in ferns and mosses, comes down in a pretty waterfall. The views from the Home Seat, and from Gill Beck Bridge, are very pleasing.

At Skyreholme, near Appletreewick, the tourist should turn aside to visit the gorge known as Troller's Gill. The way is past Skyreholme Mill dam. Dr. Whitaker thus describes this romantic spot:—"It is a winding but nearly perpendicular fissure in the limestone rock, about half-a-mile in length, a very few yards in width, and, upon an average, about 60 feet high. The bottom forms the channel of a torrent, often dry; but, when swollen by rains, devolving huge masses of limestone, which interrupt and exasperate its course. On the whole, Troller's Gill wants the waterfall, the depth and majesty of the modern Gordale (the Gordale of the modern Malham), but its general resemblance to the other, its sudden contraction and perpendicular depression, give it an exclusive claim to be the ancient Gordale of Appletreewick."

Near the Moor Cock Inn, Drygill, are the Stump Cross Caverns,—very extensive and containing stalactites of great beauty.

Appletreewick (Inns: Craven Arms and New Inn) was the birth-place of Sir William Craven, Lord Mayor of London, whose son became the first Earl of Craven. High Hall, a mansion in this parish, was the residence of Sir William.

From Barden or from Appletreewick may be made the ascent of Simon's Seat, of which the "highest point is a jagged head of grit rocks, near 1,600 feet above the sea, and probably 1,000 above the Wharfe at Appletreewick, a mile and a half off. The mighty rocks which are piled on its summit appear like some monster fortress built by giants." The view from this height is very beautiful, and extends towards the east as far as York and Ripon Minsters. Simon's Seat is also called Barden Fell East. Barden Fell West is 1,663 feet high; and these two mountains are geologically interesting as " the highest points of the mill-stone grit, in the broad ranges of that rock, east of Ryeloaf, and south of Greenhow Hill."

The river Wharfe, which has hitherto, in its downward course from Cam Fell, flowed through the mountain limestone, here, near Burnsall, enters the gritstone country; the change in the landscape is very noticeable.

Burnsall (Inn: Bridge Inn) is chiefly noticeable from the fact that it has two rectors, two rectory houses, two tithe barns, and even two pulpits. Both the medieties have, however, of late, been held by one and the same rector.

The church was restored in 1858-9; the ancient edifice was repaired in 1612, as is recorded in the following inscription, still extant:—

"This church was Repaired and Butified at thonlie costes and chardges of Sir William Craven, knight and alderm of the citie of London. And late Lord Mayre of the same, Anno dm. 1612."

Burnsall has a grammar-school.

Between Burnsall and Linton are Thorpe on the right bank and Hebden upon the left bank of the river. Those who will ramble by the river side, cross now and again the stepping-stones—locally called "hippings,"—explore the glens through which the tributary becks come down to the Wharfe, and climb the neighbouring hills, will find themselves richly rewarded by most charming scenery.

At Linton are the "Falls of the Wharfe," which, after much rain, when the river is flooded, are very fine. The falls may be viewed from the wooden bridge, supported on iron pillars, which here crosses the river. On the way to the bridge you pass the tall cotton mill and a corn mill, which is said to be one of the few "soke-mills" left in the country.

The church, which was restored in 1861-2, is a little lower down the valley. Until recently, this living was in two medieties, but by an order in council these moieties have been united.

The tourist who is acquainted with the neighbourhood of Bolton Abbey, and wishes to visit only the Upper Wharfedale, may approach the valley from Skipton, by way of Rylstone. The road, leaving Flasby Fell and Rylstone Fell on the right, passes through the village of Rylstone. Of Rylstone Hall nothing now remains, but some ruins of Norton Tower may still be seen upon the fell. This district has been rendered familiar to the reader of Wordsworth by the references to it in that charming poem, "The White Doe of Rylstone." Canto fifth opens with this stanza:—

> "High on a point of rugged ground,
> Among the wastes of Rylstone Fell,
> Above the loftiest ridge or mound,
> Where foresters or shepherds dwell,
> An edifice of warlike frame
> Stands single—Norton Tower its name—
> It fronts all quarters, and looks around,
> O'er path and road, o'er plain and dell,
> Dark moor, and gleam of pool and stream,
> Upon a prospect without bound."

The road next passes the village of Cracoe, and then approaches the valley of the Wharfe, either by Linton or Threshfield. The bridge—a handsome and massive bridge of five arches—is then crossed, and Grassington, on the other side of the river, is reached, after a journey from Skipton of between 10 and 11 miles.

Grassington (Inns: Jobbers' Arms, Devonshire Arms, Foresters' Arms, and Black Horse) is a little town which has its fairs and its annual "feast." Its importance is chiefly owing, however, to the extensive and profitable lead mines which are distant two or three miles from the town, and which those who are interested in such matters will do well to visit from here. There is a fine old bridge at Grassington, which, it is said, is the only bridge over the Wharfe which has not at some period been washed away by the impetuous stream.

Threshfield is on the right bank of the river, and has a grammar school, where the learned Dr. Whitaker, the historian of Craven, received his education as a boy.

Between Threshfield and Gordale, in a remote spot, are the remains of what is called "The Druids' Circle."

The walk of about three miles from Grassington to Coniston is very pleasant. On the way the tourist should pause to view the rapids known as Ghaistrill Force and Ghaistrill Strid, should linger amid the floral wealth of Grass Wood, or the stunted but beautiful timber of Bastow Wood, and, better still, should climb to the summit of Dew Bottom Scar, whence is a magnificent prospect, or should make a detour to Trumla Ha' and Dib Scar Glen.

At Coniston, half-way between Grassington and Kettlewell, i a church, which has been recently restored, and which contains some Norman portions, that have been preserved with due care.

The visitor will, however, cross the river by the substantial bridge, for the great attraction of this part of the dale is on the western side;— we refer to Kilnsey Scar.

Kilnsey (Inns: Tennant's Arms and Anglers' Inn) is a prettily situated village, where the pedestrian may halt for the night.

Kilnsey Scar or Crag is a cliff of limestone, about 165 feet in height, and extending nearly half-a-mile. The summit overhangs to a distance of something like 40 feet. It is a remarkably fine scar viewed from below; though less imposing than Malham Cove, and without the interest given by the river which issues from the foot of that glorious precipice, Kilnsey, with its beetling top, its ledges and its fissures, and its bold surface, here grey with lichen, and there green with ivy and with bushes, has a grandeur and a beauty of its own.

The Scar may be climbed at the side. Startling on your way rabbits from the bushes and goats upon the crags, you may, without much labour, reach the summit, and you will be rewarded by charming views both up and down the valley.

The first impression that such scars as Kilnsey give you is, that they are sea-cliffs; and this is the conclusion of modern science. "The great inland cliffs," says Professor Phillips, "which are among the most striking phenomena of Yorkshire, only differ from sea-cliffs because the water no longer beats against them. The Hambledon Hills, the Wolds, no less than Giggleswick Scar, were cliffs against a wide sea. Kilnsey Crag was a promontory overlooking the primæval sea-loch, which is now the green valley of the Wharfe; and the mural precipices which gird the bases of Whernside, Ingleborough, and Pennegent, formed the bold margin to similar branches of the sea which extended up Chapel-le-dale and Ribblesdale."

It was to Kilnsey that the vast flocks of sheep belonging to the monks of Fountains Abbey, which were pastured upon the fells in this district, were annually driven to be shorn. "The bleating of the sheep," says Whitaker, "the echoes of the surrounding rocks, the picturesque habits of the monks, the uncouth dress, long beards and cheerful countenances of the shepherds, the bustle of the morning and the good cheer of the evening, would, altogether, form a picture and a concert to which nothing in modern appearances or living manners can be supposed to form any parallel."

From Kilnsey the pedestrian may visit Dowker-bottom, or Dowker-bottom Cave, at a distance of about two miles. It will be well to take a guide, as the place is not easy to find. The stalactites in this cave have been to a large extent destroyed; but at any time the designation, "the miniature Antiparos," must have been an exaggeration. There are, however, two fine chambers. In this cave have been found human skeletons and various relics—pottery and Roman coins —indicating that, like the Victoria Cave, near Settle, this was a retreat for British refugees. The bones of wild animals found there prove that it was at a very remote time the home of the deer, the wolf, and other beasts. The cave has been examined by Mr. Jackson, Mr. Denny, Mr. Farrer, and others given to the explorations now known as "cave hunting."

A little above Kilnsey is the confluence of the Skirfare with the Wharfe, and the junction of Littondale with Kettlewelldale —as our valley is called hereabout.

Littondale,—formerly called Amerdale,—

"The deep fork of Amerdale."—WORDSWORTH.

is a charming secluded valley, which the admirer of the remoter and more primitive dales of Yorkshire will do well to explore to its head.

The hamlet of Hawkswick is passed on the way up the valley towards Arncliffe.

Arncliffe is the most important village in this valley; and indeed the parish of Arncliffe includes all Littondale. The church has been restored, and is well cared for.

Beyond, and nearer the head of the valley, is Litton; and still higher, is Halton Gill. From Litton a road leads by Nether Hesleden, Over Hesleden, Pennegent House and Stainforth to Settle. From Halton Gill is a mountain path to Raisgill, in Langstrothdale. From Arncliffe is a mountain path over Horse's Head to Hubberholme, a distance of about five miles.

Kettlewell (Inn: Marshall's) is a small market town inhabited largely by lead miners, and altogether a primitive little settlement. It is a place of some local importance, has three fairs a year, and gives its name to this portion of the valley of the Wharfe. The river, in its descent from the source to this point falls a depth of about 600 feet! There was formerly a small Norman church in this parish; the present is a modern one, containing, however, a relic of the old edifice in a curious cylindrical Norman font.

Near Kettlewell are Dove Cove and Douk Cave —the latter is worth a visit.

From Kettlewell may be made the ascent of two great mountains: one, "the weather-beaten Whernside, at whose foot it stands; the best time for which is in August, when the heather is in bloom and the grouse are on the wing;" the other, Buckden Pike. There is a road through the pass between these heights, which leads through Coverdale to Middleham in Wensleydale.

Still ascending the valley, passing Starbottom, we come to Buckden (Inns: Cock, and Buck) which is the terminus of the Wharfedale omnibus which daily conveys the "royal mail" from Skipton, and daily performs the return journey down the dale. From this point a road leads northwards by Bishopdale into Wensleydale, which is touched at Aysgarth,—a large village four miles below Bainbridge.

Buckden is in a sheltered nook at the angle here formed by the course of the Wharfe; there are some good houses in the neighbourhood. The beauty of the country has been improved by recent plantations of fir trees, for which thanks must be rendered to the Hon. Mrs. Ramsden.

Above Buckden the valley of the Wharfe is termed Langstrothdale, usually pronounced Langsterdale. Ascending the dale, the traveller first reaches Hubberholme, where is a church with very ancient portions, and a rood-loft dated 1558, —the year of Queen Mary's death. The church was restored in 1863.

Langstrothdale is believed to be the "toun," that "hight Strother, ffer in the north," whence came the Cambridge scholars of whom we read in Chaucer's Reve's Tale. The story is considered to abound in samples of the dialect peculiar to this part of Craven.

Above Hubberholme is Raisgill, and above this, Yockenthwaite; and then successively Deepdale and Beckermonds, at the confluence of Outershaw Beck and Greenfield Beck. The remotest hamlet is Outershaw, near which, on the slope of Cam Fell, is the source of the river Wharfe.

On these moors abound the scarlet cloud-berries, or nout-berries, —berries larger than raspberries, but of a sickly taste, which are used by the people for tarts and puddings.

After tracing the Wharfe to its source, we can sympathize with the enthusiasm of the native of this romantic country, (Mr. B. J. Harker) who thus apostrophizes his beloved stream :--

    Oh! deer owd Wharfe, sa clear and breet,
      That I cud hear thee merrie sang,
    An' ligg me on thee banks sa sweet,
      Or wander by thee aw day lang.

    I'd watch thee bonnie speckled fish
      Sieze on the May-flee at a spring;
    An' view thee watters aw sa lish,
      Bound frae the rocks, an' perlies fling.

    An' now it maks my heart run hee
      To think o' thease hours, tho' past;
    An' till ha dee, I'll thankful be,
      Me lot be Wharfe wer ivver cast.

CHAPTER IV.

Malham and Gordale.

Inns:—The Buck, and Lister's Arms.

ONE of the most interesting and delightful excursions to be made in Craven, and indeed in England, is that to Malham Cove and Gordale Scar. These wonderful productions of Nature in her sublimest moods may best be visited from the railway station at Bell Busk, although it is quite feasible to drive either from Skipton or from Settle. The landlord of the Buck, if a letter be sent to him beforehand, will send a trap to the Bell Busk station to meet the train. But we will presume the visitor to be a pedestrian, and for his benefit, we will describe our own visit.

Leaving the station, we entered a gate and passed through a farm-yard. Assured that the "road was good enough to find," we pursued a footpath which led us sometimes across the fields and sometimes through shady lanes, until we struck the carriage road, near Airton. In the neighbourhood of Airton are Calton Hall and Scotsthrop. From this hamlet, which, as its name indicates, is on the banks of the new-born river Aire, it is possible to proceed either by high road or footpath. For ourselves, we never hesitate when this alternative is offered. We turned into the footpath near the cotton mill, and pursued the course of the mill-stream, and then of the river. We found it a pretty walk, commanding fine views of the hills we were approaching, and the great "Craven fault," as it is termed by geologists, which is so conspicuous a feature of this district. A pleasant path it is by the gleaming, prattling stream; now a pair of kingfishers darted across the brook into the bushes, anon an angler threw his fly to tempt the wary trout; the cattle gathered beneath the shade of the ash trees in the pastures; the lark carolled in the heavens; so the way seemed short to the stone bridge over the river at Hanlith, where, turning from the mansion and park on the slope above, we admired the view of Kirkby Malham, and its church tower and houses among the trees.

Instead of continuing along the path by the river we bent our steps towards Kirkby. Amidst the grey old houses, dating from the early part of the 17th century,—of which there are but a few in the village—is the large church, the "kays" of which were duly procured for us. Its architecture is mainly Perpendicular. Upon entering the nave the first things that struck us were the niches in the west sides of the columns,—evidently prepared for small statues, and two old corbels of a grotesque character, above two of the arches. The pews in this church are of the true old-fashioned family type; we never saw so many square oak pews, with initials and dates carved upon their backs. One is dated 1631, and another 1649, and not a few of the owners have described themselves and their quality by their initials followed by the important letters, ESQ There is a handsome old font of round shape, with dog-tooth moulding, probably Norman, and a massive old oak chest. We were interested and amused by two frescoes which have been brought to light upon the west wall; one of them representing a skeleton, and the other a winged figure,—marvellous specimens of art

The chief interest of the church lies in its connection with the Lambert family, whose most distiugnished member was the Major-General Lambert of the Parliamentary army. There is a mural monument to the son, and a brass plate to the memory of the grandson of the famous republican officer. We climbed to the belfry, and upon looking at the three bells descried an inscription upon the largest, which runs thus:— "JOSIAS LAMBERT, 1602. GOD SAVE OUR CHURCH, OUR QUEEN, AND REALM." From this it appears that the Lamberts were loyal enough to the throne in the days of Queen Bess, and were driven into rebellion—if it is to be so called—by the arbitrary acts and perfidious character of Charles I. From the top of the steeple we enjoyed a pretty and varied view of Malham-dale and its encompassing hills. On leaving the church we noticed what seemed to be the fragment of an old coffin-lid, of stone, with handsome cross decorations, let into the wall of the porch, and in the church-yard the fragments of a dilapidated sun-dial.

Perhaps the greatest curiosity of Kirkby Malham is the signature of Oliver Cromwell in the parish registers. The following is an extract, with a fac-simile of the Protector's autograph annexed:—

"The intended marriage between Martine Knowles, of "Middle House, in the p'ishe of Kirkbiemalhamdale, and "Dorothy Hartley, of West Marton, in the p'ishe of Marton, "was published three severall market dayes in the open "markett place att Settle; that is to say upon the 4th of "December the first tyme, and on the 11th of December the "second tyme, and on the 18th of December the third tyme, "1655. And the said Martine Knowles and Dorothy Hartley "was married the 17th of January, 1656, in the p'sence of "these witnesses, Henry Mitchell younger, of Marton, and "Anthony Hartley, of West Marton, and others before mee,"

Oliver Cromwell Reg

(Viz.: Registered.)

Our preference for a footpath inclined us, when a little way out of the village, to turn by a stile on the right into the fields. The path we took soon joined that which we had left at Hanlith, and led us past a cotton mill, through the valley by the brook, where limestone scars rise upon the right, until we came to Malham.

Entering the village by the Wesleyan Chapel, and passing the Buck Inn, we kept to the left where the road forks, and following a lane bordered with sycamores and ashes, soon found ourselves in the open country. Many years before we had made a pilgrimage to Malham Cove, and we were wondering whether our recollections of its grandeur were coloured to any extent by youthful imagination. As we turned into the pastures, at the second gate on the right, we were not charmed by the view of the ugly stone walls dividing the hill-side before us into unshapely fields. However, we passed through the coppice of hazel, ash, and thorn, which borders the brook in the valley, and presently stood in front of and below the majestic cliffs. No! old impressions were not unjust: for sublimity and beauty combined, few scenes in England can rival Malham Cove. Before us rose an amphitheatre of white limestone, the summit of which is 470 yards in breadth, stained with grey and brown and black, and towering to a height of 286 feet! Running partially across its front are vast jutting ledges of rock, clothed with grass and shrubs and trees, and projecting so far as to cast a shadow upon the rock beneath.

At the base of this prodigious cliff the river Aire issues from the subterraneous darkness into the light of day. Where the rock is stained a vivid green with living mosses, and dyed yellow and orange with the brilliant lichen, the pellucid water flows into the sedgy pools and over the rocky bed. The shimmer of sun-light was on the running, rippling water current, and was reflected upon the rock which overhangs the source, in a dancing, fairy-like shiver. Sitting under the shadow of an ash tree, in that quiet August noon, as the breeze stirred the boughs above us, we gazed upwards to the lofty scar, watched the swallows dart from their holes in the rocks and soar and whirl in swift and graceful flight. How grandly the white masses of cloud come moving over the summit of the craggy cliff! How sweetly, as the brook murmurs on its way, and the soft air stirs in the boughs, is the soul possessed with "the melody of woods, and winds, and waters!"

Turn from the majesty above to the loveliness around; admire the modest cranes-bill at your feet; let your eye take in the scene in all its richness and its beauty—the plumy, nodding grasses, the glancing stream, the moss-stained rocks, the rude and lichened walls, the stately fern frond, the fluttering butterfly, the water-hen startled in her haunt, chuckling as she flies down the rivulet, and vanishes into the hazel copse!"

It is upon record that on rare occasions the waters of Malham Tarn have overflowed this prodigious precipice. As the height of the cliff is about double that of the famous Fall of Niagara, it may be imagined how glorious a scene such a catastrophe must present. Thomas Hurtley, of Malham, writing in 1786, says:—"From the apex of this Cove, after what is in this part called "a rugg," or a succession of rainy and tempestuous weather, when the water-sink at the southern extremity of the Tarn is unable to receive the overflux of the lake, there falls a large and heavy torrent, making a more grand and magnificent cascade than imagination can form an idea of."

After luncheon at the inn, we set off for Gordale Scar. Following the road leading eastward from the fork in the hamlet, in about a mile we reached a farm-yard on the left, through which we passed, and guided by the course of the brook, soon reached the famous gorge. The rocks soon close in on either hand, terraced with grassy slopes between the ledges,—old yews and other trees springing from their sides. Where the chasm commences, the rocks, which are 300 feet in height, become precipitous and soon overhang the narrow entrance below. Those on the right over-arch in a way which is imposing and terrific—they are said to project nearly 60 feet. Scrambling over rough stones embedded in the soil, we arrived at the foot of the fall. Standing under the right hand crag, which, with its beetling mass, threatens to overwhelm the whole gorge, we looked up towards the fall. The stream from the moors above comes hurtling down this frightful cleft, pours its water through an immense natural arch of rock, 8 feet high by 15 feet long, through which you catch a glimpse of the sun-light on the rocky piles towering behind and above, and then plunges adown the chasm in a succession of most beautiful cascades.

The young and active may easily ascend the Scar by crossing the stream to the other bank, and climbing up the face of the rock by the aid of foot-holes which have been worn in the nearly perpendicular face of the limestone rock. The views on the ascent and from the summit will well repay the toil. Altogether, Gordale Scar offers a scene of surprising wildness, and we cannot wonder that, to those especially whose travels have been confined to our own country, it serves as the embodiment of all their imaginations and all their dreams of grandeur and savage wildness in scenery.

The present course of the torrent dates, it is said, only from 1730, when a violent flood of water found the vent through which the mountain stream has since discharged its waters into the vale below.

Gordale should be seen, so we were told by a farmer resident in the valley, on a moonlight night during a severe frost. The enormous icicles then adorning the chasm present a spectacle of singular and romantic beauty. Probably few of our readers will have the opportunity of testing for themselves the glowing descriptions which have been given of Gordale on a frosty, moonlit evening.

Little Gordale should not be over-looked, simple as are its pretensions compared with those of its ambitious neighbour. On our way back we took a short path to the left which leads to this picturesque and peaceful spot. **Here the water falls in larger and smaller streams adown a mossy rock.** The afternoon sunlight poured through the surrounding ash trees, and glanced on the descending water, the mossy rock, and the ivied crag. The water lay beneath in a pretty and transparent pool. Passing by the stepping-stones over the current at the head of a second fall, we paused to watch its flow, as it gently stole into a wooded glen and disappeared among the overhanging ashes.

On the other side of the stepping-stones appears the mouth of a small cavern, known as Janet's Cave, which, tradition says, was formerly the abode of fairies. The spot does credit to their choice.

About two miles from Malham, on the high land above the Cove and Gordale, is Malham Tarn, the largest piece of water in Yorkshire, being about a mile across, and three miles in circumference. It is situated in a secluded and solitary region, and is 570 feet higher than the outlet of the Aire already described. Malham Water abounds in trout and perch. On its banks, and surrounded by plantations, is the seat of Colonel Morrison.

If the visitor wishes to see the Tarn and to enjoy the extensive views from the elevated ridge above both Malham Cove and Gordale Scar, he may do so by climbing the slope on the left of the Cove, making his way to Malham Water, and descending by Gordale; this he will find a walk of about three miles. In a direct line behind the Cove, will be noticed a deep and narrow pass, closed by a lofty cliff, called Coom Scar: in a flood the Tarn water not infrequently rushes over here, and forms a second Gordale, but it is commonly prevented from reaching the Cave by sinking, with singular noise and rapidity, through the shattered and fissured stratum at the foot of the pass.

Westall, Turner, and many other landscape painters, have striven to depict on canvas these glorious scenes. And poets have been inspired to sing by the high converse with Nature they have enjoyed among these limestone scars and caves.

Even although Wordsworth's sonnets on these grand works of the great Artificer are said to have been inspired by pictures, and not by the realities, we think the reader will be pleased to have them before his eyes when he is visiting the spots to which they refer.

MALHAM COVE.

"Was the aim frustrated by force or guile,
 When giants scooped from out the rocky ground,
 Tier under tier, this semicirque profound?
 (Giants!—the same who built on Erin's isle
 That Causeway, with incomparable toil!)
 O! had this vast theatric structure wound
 With finished sweep into a perfect round;
 No mightier work had gained the plausive smile
 Of all beholding Phœbus! But, alas,
 Vain earth! false world! foundations must be laid
 In Heaven; for 'mid the wreck of *is* and *was*,
 Things incomplete, and purposes betrayed,
 Make sadder transits o'er thought's optic glass
 Than noblest objects utterly decayed."

GORDALE SCAR.

"At early dawn, or rather when the air
 Glimmers with fading light, and shadowy Eve
 Is busiest to confer and to bereave;
 Then, pensive Votary! let thy feet repair
 To Gordale chasm, terrific as the lair
 Where the young lions couch; for so, by leave
 Of the propitious hour, thou may'st perceive
 The local Deity, with oozy hair,
 And mineral crown, beside his jagged urn
 Recumbent; Him thou may'st behold, who hides
 His lineaments by day, yet there presides,
 Teaching the docile waters how to turn,
 Or, (if need be) impediment to spurn,
 And force their passage to the salt-sea tides!"

The reader will be interested in reading the language in which the poet Gray, who visited Gordale in 1769, recorded the impression the scene produced upon him:—

"As I advanced," he says, "the crags seemed to close in,
"but discovered an entrance to the left between them; I
"followed my guide a few paces, and the hills opened again
"into no large space; and then all further way is barred by a
"stream, that at the height of about 50 feet, gushes from a
"hole in the rock, and spreading its large sheets over its
"broken front, dashes from step to step, and then rattles away
"in a torrent down the valley; the rock on the left rises
"perpendicular, with stubbed yew trees and shrubs starting
"from its sides, to the height of at least 300 feet. But these
"are not the thing; it is the rock on the right, under which
"we stand to see the fall, that forms the principal horror of

"the place. From its very base it begins to slope forwar'
"over you in one black and solid mass, without any crevice
"in its surface, and overshadows half of the area below
"in its dreadful canopy. When I stood, I believe, four
"yards from its foot, the drops which perpetually distil from
"its brow, fell upon my head, and in one part of its top,
"more exposed to the weather, there are loose stones that
"hang in the air, and threaten visibly some idle spectator
"with instant destruction; it is safer to shelter yourself close
"to its bottom and trust to the mercy of that enormous mass,
"which nothing but an earthquake can stir. The gloomy
"uncomfortable day well suited the savage aspect of the
"place, and made it still more formidable. I staid there, not
"without shuddering, a quarter of an hour, and thought
"my trouble richly repaid, for the impression will last with
"life."

There are several ways of walking from Malham to Settle; but we warn the pedestrian that no road will be found short, or perfectly easy to find. To describe our own route: turning westward at the bottom of the hamlet, we followed an old green lane, and then a footpath, at first indistinct, but afterwards clearly marked enough, until near some fir plantations on high ground we reached the mountain road leading from Kirkby Malham. From this point we had not the slightest difficulty in finding the way. The road crosses the shoulder of High Side, and is comparatively little used on account of its steepness at either end; for we met not a solitary wayfarer, startling only the grouse or the lapwing on the moor. There are fine views all the way, first down Airedale, then across the plain to Pendle Hill. In the middle of the moor the road divides; one track leads to Kirkby, another to Airton, the third—*i.e.*, our road—to Settle. This road leads by Scaleber and under Attermire, and descends near Castleberg into Settle. But we found it a good three hours' walk from Malham to the old Settle Station; in fact it was only by dint of a hard run the last two miles that we saved the last train to Clapham, and our dinner at the "Flying Horse Shoe."

From Malham, the pedestrian who wishes to visit Wharfedale, may find his way, over the moors and mountains, to Threshfield, a distance of seven miles, or to Kilnsey, a distance of eight miles.

CHAPTER V.

Settle and Giggleswick.

Inns:—Golden Lion, Commercial, Royal Oak, White Horse.

When the poet Gray visited Settle in the last century, he thus described the place:—

"It is a small market town standing directly under a rocky fell; there are not above a dozen good-looking houses, and the rest are old and low, with little wooden porticoes in front."

All is changed now, except the situation, which is as pleasant and attractive as ever, and most conveniently central for the head-quarters of the tourist bent on exploring Craven and the new route to the north.

Settle is, at the present, a neat clean town, with an unmistakeable air of prosperity. The population, at the census of 1871, was 2,163, of whom 1,129 were males, and 1,034 females, showing an increase, during the decennial period, of 577. The number of houses was 420. The rateable value is £9197.

The Church of the Holy Ascension was erected in the year 1837. This is a district church—the parish church being at Giggleswick. There are places of worship for Friends, Independents, Wesleyans, and Primitive Methodists, and there is a small Roman Catholic chapel.

The Town Hall was erected in 1832, upon the site of the old Tolbooth; the style of architecture is Gothic,—not of the purest order.

There is a Literary Society which was established so long ago as the year 1770. This Society has a library in the Town Hall buildings, with upwards of 8,000 volumes. The members, who are all shareholders, number between 70 and 80.

In the Town Hall is also the Club-room of the Chess Club, which has about 40 members. The room in which chess, whist, and other games are played is well supplied with newspapers.

Settle has also, in another part of the town, a Mechanics' Hall, where is a fair library. Dr. Birkbeck, well known as the founder of Mechanics' Institutes, was born in this town, as also was Thomas Proctor, the sculptor.

There is also a Church Institute, with a reading room, library, and billiards.

It will thus be seen that provision, unusually liberal for a small town, is made for the intellectual needs and for the amusement of the population of Settle.

The fine precipice of limestone rock which rises behind Settle, to a height of 300 feet, is the most prominent attraction of the place. It is known as Castleberg, and formerly its crag served as the pointer of a sun-dial whose hours were marked along the hill-side by large stones. The grounds are kept locked, but admission is secured by a small payment. Winding paths lead through pleasant groves to the summit, whence is a fine view of Ribblesdale and the neighbouring hills. As if a fear were entertained that the scenery might be regarded as an insufficient return for the expenditure incurred at the gate of entrance, artificial attractions have been added for the benefit of the young, in the shape of swings, see-saws, and merry-go-rounds.

At the top of the town, and just below Castleberg, is a remarkable old stone house bearing the date 1679, with a very large number of mullioned windows, some square and some round headed. The house is known as "Preston's Folly," having been built by a person of that name, who, it is said, was unable to finish it. In the middle and recessed portion is the door, with singularly unique door-posts. Within, there is a fine old oak staircase. The house is now the dwelling of a farmer, and has certainly fallen from its former splendour.

Behind this house is the Castleberg Well Spring, yielding a copious flow of the clearest water.

The bridge over the Ribble, not half-a-mile from Settle, commands a very pleasing view. The singular form of Pennegent is well seen from this point. Archdeacon Paley, who received his education at Giggleswick Grammar-school, hard by, of which his father was head master, is said traditionally to have gazed on the mountain from this point, and to have likened its shape to that of a raised pie! On the banks of the river are some cotton mills.

Less than a mile from Settle, and on the opposite side of the Ribble, is the village of Giggleswick, oddly and yet prettily situated within and around a gentle hollow. A stroll about this village on a summer evening will be appreciated by the lover of English rural scenery; footpaths lead beneath stately sycamores and fragrant limes. The cottages are neat, and the gardens well cared for, and in the neighbourhood are some handsome residences, each standing within its well timbered grounds.

The Church is dedicated to an obscure patroness, St. Alkald or St. Alkilda. It is of the Perpendicular style. Upon the pulpit are carved the emblems of the 12 tribes, with their names; on the desk is the inscription:—"HEARE IS THE STANDARDES OF THE ISRAELITES WHEN THE TO CANAN CAM AGANES THE CANAANITES." There is a brass in the middle aisle to the memory of the Rev. Wm. Paley, father of the celebrated Archdeacon, who was of a Craven family, and who was for 54 years master of the grammar-school in this place.

Giggleswick School, dating from 1553, has become, of late years, one of the most important institutions of the kind in the north of England. The Board of Governors consists of the Chairman, Sir James Kaye Shuttleworth, Bart., the Vice-Chairman, Hector Christie, Esq., and fourteen other gentlemen including members of Parliament, distinguished University men, and persons of great local influence. The character of the school will be best understood from a few sentences in the "General Statement" which is prefixed to the official Class List for Midsummer, 1876:—

"In harmony with the scheme of the Endowed Schools Commission, the aim of the Governors is to provide adequate instruction in the subjects mentioned below for boys up to the age of nineteen who intend to proceed from school to the Universities, to compete for appointments in the Civil Service, or to pass the Entrance Examinations for the army; also to provide more completely than has been usual for the education of those who wish to qualify themselves at school for their business or profession.

"The intention of the Governors is that Giggleswick should be a first-grade modern school, that is a school answering in every respect to a first-grade classical school, except that the leading subjects of instruction are Latin, Modern Languages and Literature, Natural Science and Mathematics. Greek except in special cases, and Verse Composition, are omitted.

"The whole internal organization, management, and discipline of the school is in the hands of the Head Master.

"Religious instruction is given generally throughout the school in accordance with the teaching of the Church of England. But special exemptions are made upon the application of parents."

Great attention is paid to Chemistry and the various branches of Physics. The Governors have appropriated over £2,000 to the erection of the Laboratory, and the Lecture room, and the provision of apparatus.

The arrangements for Boarders are worthy of note.

"The Governors of the School have recently expended a sum of about £20,000 in building a large Boarding House or Hostel, in providing Masters' Houses, and other buildings. The Hostel resembles the most convenient boarding houses at the best large English schools, containing numerous studies for the elder boys, and dormitories so arranged that each boy has a separate compartment. According to the Hostel system the general management is in the hands of the Governing Body, so that it is not an object to the Master that profit should be made from Boarders. There is at present excellent accommodation for about 130 Boarders."

Large additions have recently been made to the school buildings. It is evident that the public appreciate the unusual advantages of the school, especially the liberality and breadth of the education given, and the moderation of the terms.

The present Head Master is the Rev. George Style, M.A., Fellow of Queen's College, Cambridge.

Beyond the village the road skirts what is known as Giggleswick Scar. This is a range of limestone cliffs, which marks the Craven Fault,—a vast displacement of strata of the highest geological interest. The visitor will find this walk below the Scar one extremely agreeable. The bold rocks are ornamented with ivy and the indigenous yew, and beneath, the fir plantations and hazel trees clothe the broken and stony ground.

There are several caves among these scars, of which the most interesting are the Dangerous and the Staircase Caves.

But the chief feature of interest in this excursion is the celebrated Ebbing and Flowing Well. This is a spring of an intermittent character, which flows at irregular intervals into a stone basin by the road-side. The visitor may wait for hours and fail to see the performance, or it may chance to occur more than once during his inspection. In very wet or very dry weather it does not usually display its peculiarities so freely as in seasons of moderate rain. Drayton, in the Polyolbion, describes the fountain as 'sometime a nymph,'—

"——Among the mountains high
Of Craven, whose blue heads for caps put on the sky."

Flying from a satyr she was changed into a spring; and—

" Even as the fearful nymph then thick and short did blow,
Now made by them a spring, so doth she ebb and flow."

Modern Science gives a less poetic explanation of this peculiarity. The curious intermittent action designated ebbing and flowing is due to the singular passage of the water through the channels and reservoirs in the limestone rock; syphon-like conduits of a natural character seem to connect the chambers in which the water is stored. Variable pressure upon the water in the interior, occasioned by diminished or augmented rainfall, produces in this manner what appear to be capricious ebbings and flowings. This solution, upon the principle of the double syphon, was first given, it is believed, by the late Thomas Hargreaves, of Settle, whose explanatory model may be seen in the Library of the Institute at Settle.

The accompanying wood-cut will render this interesting phenomenon easy of comprehension:--

A, the great basin formed in the rock. B, the duct that conveys the water to C, the smaller basin. D, the duct that conveys the water from C to E, the well. F, crevices through which the water escapes into the duct D when the stream is not sufficient to fill the duct B. G, crevices through which the water escapes from A to C, when A is overcharged. It will be seen that B and D form each a syphon; B draws off the water from the basin A, and fills the smaller basin C until it runs over at D; now D being wider than B soon empties the basin C, and then the stream ceases until C is filled up again, thus causing the reciprocation.

The irregularity of the reciprocation is caused thus: B draws off the water from A faster than it is supplied by the spring, consequently A becomes empty, and no reciprocation takes place until it is filled again to the height of the syphon B, when the fulness of A causes a most powerful one, and before the well goes down to its proper medium, another, but less powerful one, takes place, and the interval between each flux and reflux increases, until A is emptied again. In dry weather there is no reciprocation, because the water is insufficient to fill B, and it escapes through the crevices F; and after much rain the basin C is too powerfully supplied by B and the crevices G.

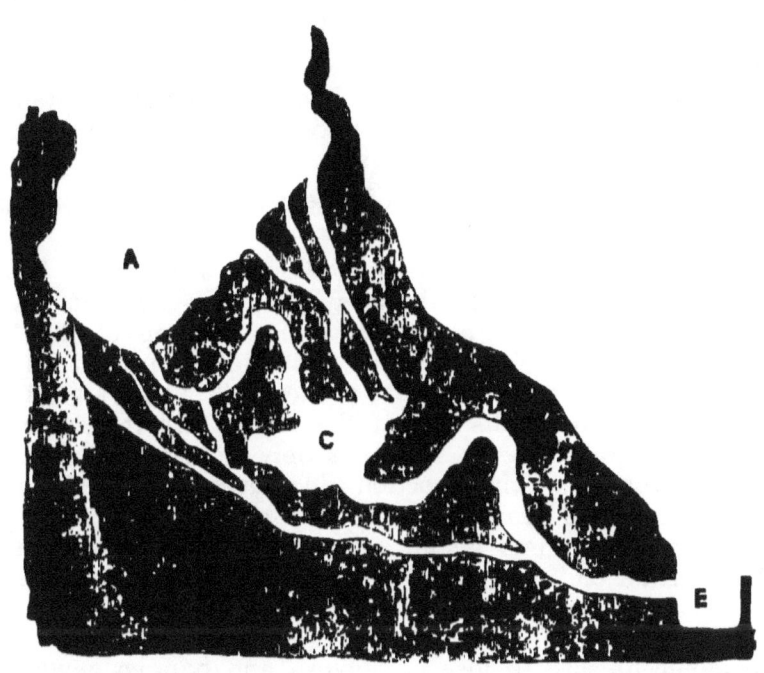

From Giggleswick Well, the visitor may climb the steep hill above, called Buckhaw Brow, and thence to the summit of the Ox Scar, whence a grand view may be enjoyed. Turning eastward, he may reach Ribblesdale at Stackhouse or at Little Stainforth.

Above Stackhouse is a Cairn 80 feet in diameter, in which human bones have been found.

Robin Hood's Mill is the name given to a spot between Little Stainforth and Stackhouse, where a rumbling noise may be heard below the ground, doubtless caused by a subterranean waterfall, such as are not uncommon in this district.

Stainforth is a pretty village on the Ribble. Below the bridge between Great and Little Stainforth, is Stainforth Foss or Force, where the river, amidst beautiful surrounding scenery, rushes down a contracted channel. The view at this spot is one that should not be missed.

On the Cowside Beck, which falls into the Ribble at Stainforth, is Catterick or Catrigg Foss, where the mountain stream descends the glen in a cascade of six or seven falls.

The return to Settle is by Langcliffe, where is a modern church, and in the middle of the valley a large cotton (doubling) mill.

Langcliffe Hall is said to have been occasionally visited by Sir Isaac Newton, who was on intimate terms with the then owner of the hall,—Major Dawson.

One of the finest walks from Settle is that over the mountains to Malham.

The hills behind Castleberg are easily accessible. There is a narrow road from Settle, by which the pedestrian leaves Castleberg on the right and so gains the top of the hill. There is a second road by which Castleberg is passed on the left. There are splendid views of the south and west all the way up, and from the top of the ridge. By the mountain roads Malham is five or six miles only from Settle; Gordale is a mile further. The direction given us by a native was:— " Take the road leaving Castleberg on the left, climb the hill, and when some distance beyond it climb the 'bits of hills' further on." Walter White seems to have undertaken the journey upon some such directions as these:—" an old man who was passing strongly urged us to keep the road; we should be sure to lose ourselves, 'and happen never get to Maum at all.'" However, though in some doubt when in sight of Stockdale, by keeping toward the east he found his way. Not every traveller afoot, it should be said, has the genial "Londoner's" notion of going across country.

Another excursion from Settle may be made to Long Preston, where is a fifteenth century church; and to Hellifield, which boasts a "peel," or square tower, built by Lawrence Hamerton in the nineteenth year of Henry VI. On the other side of the river from Long Preston is Wigglesworth, (Inn: The Plough), where are the remains of an ancient hall, and where are sulphurous and chalybeate springs, which capricious Fortune has not been pleased to raise to the reputation of Harrogate or Tunbridge Wells.

Distances from Settle :—To Malham by mountain road, 6 miles; by Hellifield 14 miles; to Long Preston, 4 miles; to Horton, 6 miles;. to Clapham, 6 miles; to Ingleton 10 miles.

Spa Well, Wigglesworth.

CHAPTER VI.

Scaleber, Attermire, and the Victoria Cave.

ONE of the most interesting and enjoyable excursions that can be made from Settle is that to the mountains immediately behind the town. The walk which we are about to describe is one that can be accomplished easily in four hours, allowing time for resting, for admiring the waterfall, and for inspecting the Cave.

We took the mountain-road to Malham at the upper part of the town, and with a little steep climbing soon found ourselves on high ground overlooking the valley. Following this road for a mile and somewhat more, we came to a bridge which crosses a mountain torrent. Instead of crossing this bridge, we turned over a stile to the right and a few steps brought us within view of Scaleber Force.

This is a cascade of great beauty; the stream falls down the slope of a mossy rock, and presently vanishes in a thickly wooded glen.

This walk might be prolonged to the summit of Rye-loaf, a a brown and rounded mountain commanding an extensive view. But we retraced our steps until we came to the road which leads to Stockdale. From this road we turned off by a stile on the left. Here we paused to enjoy a singularly beautiful prospect. Before us stood a green mound known as Sugar-loaf, or Salt-pie; beyond, a magnificent assemblage of rocks and cliffs: on the left, a mountain with craggy escarpments, and crowned by a cairn: to the right, a succession of low, broken, rounded summits; and still more to the right, less broken and more even hill-tops, yet supported by perpendicular precipices. The entrances to the Attermire and other caves may be seen from this spot; the Victoria Cave is hidden.

Advancing, we crossed the site of an ancient mere, from which it has been surmised that the place derived its name—Otter-mere, corrupted into Attermire. We made for a gate near the butts which are used by the North Craven Rifles for their practice. We then ascended a rugged path, leaving several hills known as Warrendale Knots and Beacon Scar (Ben Scar) on the left, and Attermire Scar on the right, and skirting along the base of Brentscar soon arrived at the entrance to the Victoria Cave, which may be recognized by the mass of *débris* on the slope below the approach. A glorious point of view it is! And, though the ancient British dwellers took refuge in this lovely spot for safety, and not for the sake, certainly, of any picturesqueness in the views commanded from this mountain abode, we could not but reflect that the same prospect stretched before their eyes, which we, in happier circumstances, were now surveying. In front is Brent Scar. Looking to the left, over Barnoldswick and over Gargrave, over Warrendale Knots towers Pendle Hill, near which on a clear day, with the help of a glass, may be discerned the town of Clitheroe. To the right is the valley of the Wenning, and beyond, that of the Lune. Ingleton is visible over Stackhouse; Bentham lies in the valley, and beyond is Bowlands. Still farther, are the hills about Lancaster, and a little more to the right, the summits of the more southerly mountains of the Lake district heave in view. Just below us is Ribblesdale, with Moughton Fell rising as its western boundary. Looking more to the right, we see Ingleton Fells, and on the extreme right the long flat summit of Ingleborough.

The Victoria Cave is situated about a mile and a half from Settle, in a north-easterly direction, at an elevation of about 900 feet above the town and the river Ribble, and 1440 feet above the sea-level. We will tell the story of its discovery, as told us by the discoverer himself,—Mr. Joseph Jackson.

"It was," said he, "in the year 1838, the year of Queen Victoria's coronation, that the cave was first discovered. It was this that led to its being named 'The Victoria Cave.' A dog was really the first discoverer; he went into a hole of the rock and came out at another place This aroused my curiosity. Entering in with some difficulty, I found that I was in a cave, but a cave filled up nearly to the top. Creeping on, however, I found it more lofty than at the entrance. The roof was hung with stalactites, and the surface was covered with bones of recent animals. Looking among the bones, I discovered a coin, in a part of the cave where water drips in. It was plain, therefore, that the cave contained remains of the presence, not only of brutes, but of man. These chance finds led to a search, and to the consequent discovery, not only of bones and teeth, but of coins and other relics of human occupation. At that time we worked to a depth of two feet; and nothing, in the shape of bronzes and other antiquities, was found at a greater depth than this.

"In the year 1870 a Committee was formed thoroughly to explore the cave by digging and removing the contents to a depth of six feet throughout. Here we discovered many Roman antiquities. In digging a shaft near the entrance of the cave, we met with bones of extinct animals, at a depth of about 25 feet below the surface. At a greater depth than this nothing was found. As we advanced farther into the interior they were met with at a depth not exceeding 15 feet.

"We have found teeth or bones of elephant, rhinoceros, three kinds of bears, hyæna, bison, reindeer, wolf, andhippopotamus. A bone, said by high authorities to be that of a man, was found along with those of the extinct animals.

"The explorations are still going on under the direction of a scientific committee. I am superintendent of the work, and am there usually every day. The expenses are met by a grant from the British Association, and by public subscription."

The bulk of the bones which have been discovered, and many of the antiquities, are deposited in the museum of Giggleswick School, and can be seen by application to the Head Master.

Some few of the Roman remains are in the British Museum.

Mr. Jackson, who resides at Settle, has himself a small but highly interesting collection of relics of antiquity, discovered in the Victoria and other caves, which, on the occasion of our visit, he courteously permitted us to inspect. Among the many objects of interest this collection contains, we especially noticed the following : of *stone*, several whetstones,—both round and pyramidical,—some fine round sling stones, a variety of flint instruments, several discs (of uncertain use), spindle-whorls, chert implements of different kinds. In some of these implements are circular holes, the splayed form of which seems to indicate that they were drilled with a blunt tool. Of *bone*, many needles and pins of primitive forms, what appear to be handles pierced in the centre, bone fibulæ or dress fasteners, arrow-heads and arrow-tips, shuttles, combs, fish-hooks, and spindle whorls. Of *glass*, beads of various sizes, portions of rings. (There are also beads of amber. Of *iron*, spear heads, battle-axe heads, much rusted, rings, fibulæ, and what seems to be a large key. Of *bronze*, bracelets, fiibulæ, ornaments, and various fragments. Of *lead*, some pierced discs. Of *silver*, a circular-headed or ornamented pin. There is also a small enamelled ring.

This collection also contains a few coins of much interest. One bears on the obverse, "CONSTANTINUS MAX. AUG." The reverse bears the legend "EXERCITUS," with the monogram Constantine adopted after his conversion, compounded of the initial letters in Greek of the name, Christ. This coin is believed to have been struck at Constantinople. Another orass coin is Hadrian's, between A.D. 117—138. It bears the head of that emperor, with the face to the right. The inscription in full reads, "IMP. CÆSAR TRAJANUS HADRIANUS AUG. P. M. T. R. Cos. III." Reverse, "MONETA AVGVSTI, S. C." Another coin is a third brass of Aurelian, between A.D. 270—275. It bears on the obverse "IMP. AURELIANUS AUG.," with the head of the emperor to the right, with diadem and cuirass; on the reverse, as nearly as can be made out, is the sun, with two captives at his feet, and "ORIENS AUG. XXI "

To return to our excursion:—The old entrance to the cave we saw upon our left, above us At the opening the cave is nearly 100 feet in width, and is now about 32 feet in height from the bottom to the top.

We soon found the sticky clay anything but an agreeable carpet to the cave, and could have wished a pavement of the stalagmite which was found in layers with clay above and below it. The workmen were engaged in cutting and blasting a more commodious roadway into the interior of the cave. With their help, and by the light of candles, we explored the more accessible parts of this singularly interesting cavern.

Chamber D is distinguished by a dome which rises, as a kind of architectural feature, above the rest of the cave. In this chamber were found bones in great numbers and variety, —269 specimens for the year 1875 having been classified by Professor Busk.

We next penetrated the Birkbeck Gallery, which extends to a distance of 112 feet from the above-mentioned dome. It is a long gallery, with holes or drops, which make it no easy work to proceed to the extremity. A glazy moist stalactite covers the walls. On the right, before entering the gallery, is a small passage or hole, where bones were found.

Returning from the Birkbeck Gallery, we entered chamber B, which is the finest in the cave This chamber is, with A, upon the left as you enter. Water lies in the bottom, where a shaft was sunk from above to a depth of 25 feet. The stalagmite in this chamber was six feet in thickness.

Chambers A and B were the dwelling-places of the human inhabitants who, in historic times, took shelter and refuge in this strange retreat. Fancy pictured the unhappy refugees, with the relics of their civilization about them, hiding from the barbarian invader in these gloomy recesses, crouching by their wretched fires, and feeding upon the flesh of their threatened flocks and herds!

We next crept into chamber C, where is a well. In this cavity no excavations have yet been made.

An admirable and most interesting account of the Victoria Cave will be found in Mr. Boyd Dawkins' work on "Cave Hunting," pp. 81—125.

The interest of the cave is two-fold. It was the habitation of human beings in historic times. The works of art which have been discovered, and the evident traces of occupation by civilized men, have awakened speculation, which seems to lead to the conclusion that in the fifth century this cave was a place of refuge for Britons who, after the withdrawal of the Romans, were exposed to the invasions of the fierce Scots and Picts from the north, and of the Angles and Saxons from the south and east.

Mr. Boyd Dawkins says:—"The presence of these works of art, in association with the remains of the domestic animals used for food, is only to be satisfactorily accounted for in the way proposed by Mr. Dixon. Men accustomed to luxury and refinement were compelled, by the pressure of some great calamity, to flee for refuge, and to lead a half savage life in these inclement caves, with whatever they could transport thither of their property. They were also accompanied by their families, for the number of personal ornaments and the spindle whorls imply the presence of the female sex. We may also infer that they were cut off from the civilization to which they had been accustomed, since they were compelled to extemporize spindle whorls out of the vessels that they brought with them, instead of using those that had been manufactured for the purpose."

But this Cave has not merely an antiquarian, it has also a geological interest. There have been discovered in its chambers vast quantities of bones and teeth of animals of various species. These have been carefully arranged and classified, and have served as material of great value to the geologist in determining the climate of the region at various epochs, and in describing the wonderful changes which its whole aspect and its physical condition have undergone.

The fullest account of the discoveries which have taken place in the Victoria Cave, since the publication of Mr. Boyd Dawkins' work, will be found in the successive reports of Mr. R. H. Tiddeman, furnished to the British Association for the advancement of science.

One of the most noticeable among the "finds" was a bone, believed by Professor Busk to be a human fiibula, in beds considered to be pre-glacial. This discovery has been deemed important in its bearing upon the antiquity of man. The presence of man is also considered to be indicated by certain marks upon bones which, it is thought, must have been made by instruments of a rude and primitive character.

The question of greatest geological interest upon which light is believed to have been cast by the exploration of the Victoria Cave, has been thus stated:—

"Are the glacial deposits which rest upon the older bone beds, containing the extinct mammals and man, in the position which they occupied at the close of the glacial conditions, or have they subsequently fallen into their present site?" The former alternative is adopted. Mr. Tiddeman gives it as his opinion that "it is clear from the position of the boulders beneath all the screes, that they are a portion of the general glacial covering of the valleys and hill-sides which was left by the Ice Sheet at the time of its disappearance."

The ice-borne boulders in question are blocks of silurian grit and of carboniferous limestone, with one or two of carboniferous sandstone.

We returned to Settle by way of the hills over-hanging Ribblesdale, and found this an agreeable variety of route. As we neared the brow of the hill we paused to enjoy the view. Opposite us, on the other side of the valley, the hamlet of

Stackhouse nestles under Kelko Wood. Beneath us lies the village of Langcliffe, with its modern church, and its cotton mill in the middle of the valley, amongst the greenest of pastures. On the right, Ribblesdale stretches northwards towards Horton,—the carriage-road and the railroad following the course of the river. Away to the north-west rise Ingleborough, Whernside, and the fells northward to Cam Fell. Quite to the right is Stainforth, with its fine craggy Scar, and Winskill behind it; while the unmistakeable outline of Pennegent completes the charming prospect.

Warrendale Knots.

CHAPTER VII.

CLAPHAM AND INGLEBOROUGH.

Inns:—The Flying Horse Shoe, New Inn.

THERE cannot be a more desirable centre for the explorer of western Craven than the Flying Horse Shoe, at Clapham. This hostelry is close to the railway station, and is therefore conveniently situated for excursions in which the iron road may be of service. The house is a neat and unpretending one, but it affords not only accommodation but comfort in abundance. The landlord, Mr. Coates, has kept the house for 21 years, and can give every information about the country. Waggonettes, dog-carts, and flies, are to be had, as well as saddle horses and ponies. The right of showing the famous Cave is entrusted to the landlord of the inn, who can also procure guides for the ascent of Ingleborough. Parties staying in the house have the privilege of fishing in the preserved waters. A farm is attached to the inn, and the poultry-yard and dairy are consequently at the service of visitors. Ten beds are made up in the house. Distance from Settle, seven miles.

The walk from Settle and Giggleswick to Clapham is a pleasant one. Near the road are Lawkland, Feizor, Wharfe and Austwick. To the north are the slopes and rocks which form the southern boundary of the mighty Ingleborough.

Austwick has been called the "Gotham of Yorkshire." In former times, the Austwick "carles," as they were called, were credited with all the odd stories of stupidity current in Craven; they seem to have been the general butts of the wit of the country side. It was they who tried to get the bull over the gate,—who made an attempt to wall in the cuckoo,—to have fine growing spring weather all the year round,—who made an assault on a watch, "a tick 'em tack 'em fella wi' a lang tail,"—who stuck the parish whittle in the ground under a black cloud, and wanted to know where to find it next day,—who wheeled sunshine into the barn to dry the hay with,—who interpreted the gurgle of a drowning man in a pond, as "good, good, good," giving rise to the proverb, "The best at the bottom, as the Austwick carles say."

On the hill called Norber, above Austwick, there is a most remarkable group of Bowder Stones; there are several hundreds of them standing in the most eccentric postures; some are poised on single pivots, others apparently standing erect in spite of their divergence from the centre of gravity, and the outline of others bears a fantastic resemblance to some living or inanimate thing. The largest contains about four hundred cubic feet, and will therefore weigh little less than thirty tons. The crust of the hill is limestone, but below its edge may be seen the junction with the slate, the same as the Bowders. From this elevation there is an excellent view, especially along the valley which terminates in Ribblesdale, at Swarth Moor; and, in this direction, will be seen Wharfe Gill, a deep wooded glen with stream and waterfall.

A walk of about a mile and a half brings the tourist from the station to Clapham village, where is a very comfortable hotel, called the New Inn. The village is a remarkably pretty one. Clapham Beck, a bright, lively brook, runs adown through the midst, and the houses are on either side. And pretty houses they are, with their fronts covered with roses and honeysuckle. The bridge commands a charming view of the beck, as it murmurs amidst the overhanging foliage. At the top of the village, on the left of the stream, stands the church, from the pretty grave-yard of which may be seen a little waterfall, whose soothing music harmonizes with the rural, peaceful scene.

But we must not linger here; for it is to be presumed that the visitor has come to Clapham that he may see its wonderful cave.

Clapham or Ingleborough Cave is the property of James Farrer, Esq. It is guarded at the entrance by iron gates, which are kept locked. Admission is only to be obtained by application to Knowles, the appointed guide, who has filled this office for 26 years: he lives in the village, in a cottage on the south side of the river, between the bridge and the church. It is necessary to apply at the guide's house before leaving the village. Supposing that Knowles is at the cave, and you have to find your way to the cave mouth alone, you must apply to Mr. Farrer's steward for permission to walk through the private grounds. This beautiful route to the cave was formerly open to all comers, without reserve, but the privilege was on several occasions so shamefully abused that some discretion is now used in granting it. Having obtained the necessary permission, you must enter the grounds at the gate marked "Private," and keeping to the road on the left all the way you will have a charming walk of about a mile and a half to the gate which bounds these lovely grounds. You must then keep straight on along the path until you see the entrance of the cave on your left.

If you are fortunate enough to have the company of the guide through the grounds, you may perhaps get a stolen peep at a pretty little waterfall and rustic bridge which are situated near the hall.

A charge is authorised of half-a-crown for two visitors, and a shilling each for a larger party; this pays for the necessary candles and for the services of the guide.

There is no difficulty in exploring these subterraneous galleries, unless it be considered such that, in one place, it is necessary to proceed for several yards in a stooping posture. The guide advances first, and he and the members of the party are supplied with candles fixed in a kind of battledore. Here and there caution is necessary to avoid striking the head against dependent stalactites.

The cavern is in the limestone rock. The water that flows gently through its passages, and that lies in its silent pools, enters, it is believed, from the hill-side above, by a cavity in the mountain, known as "Gaping Ghyll," where a mountain stream falls into a cave 250 feet in depth. Many of the stones which lie upon the surface, and the brown sand beneath the explorer's feet, are of the mill-stone grit formation. The entire length of the cavern was, until recently, 702 yards, *i. e.*: measured to what was called the "Giant's Hall." It should be mentioned that, although what is termed the Old Hall has been known for a long time, the rest of the cavern was opened up only in 1837. But in 1872 a flood of unusual magnitude rendered the further portion of the cavern inaccessible, so that the dimensions of the present cave are far less than above mentioned.

An excellent plan of the cavern has been published, and the visitor can inspect a copy in the entrance hall of the Flying Horse Shoe. The following are the several portions as they have been named, in the order in which they occur:—After the Old Cave, the Vestibule or Eldon Hall, the Stalactite Gallery, and then the Pillar Hall. A gallery of some length then leads to the Ladies' Cushion and the First Gothic Arch. The Long Gallery, where are the Second Bells, leads to the Creeping Place, and beyond this is Grimes's Arch. The remaining portions of the cavern, as marked on the plan, are now inaccessible. Just beyond the Creeping Place is an extension to the right, which is soon found to be a *cul-de-sac*.

The stalactites and stalagmites are of varied, curious, and occasionally of beautiful character. They assume the most fantastic shapes. Here is a pair of pillars resembling the fore-legs of an elephant, there a bee-hive, and yonder a jockey's cap. An inverted forest in one part depends most gracefully from the roof; in another a bed of coral appears to be growing downwards. A massive pillar rears itself mid-way in the passage; by the wall a range of organ pipes yield excellent music in response to the strokes of the guide's staff. A fairy structure of slender columns stands in a miniature cavern, and when lights are placed behind it, is mirrored in a still, dark pool. There is "water, water, everywhere;" in one place a pool, four feet and a half in depth, reflects the candles' flame; again, the water drips swiftly from the roof; and yet again, a murmuring waterfall breaks the quiet of the scene. Dripping water is ever forming new products. In most parts of the cave old water-marks are visible, shewing the height at which the water stood before the opening up of the cave. The visitor is thus reminded what gentle, but mighty force it was, that shaped this wondrous, winding cavern beneath the massive mountain.

A curious experiment was made by Mr. Farrer, to determine the length of time occupied in the very gradual formation of the stalagmites. The "Jockey Cap" was selected for the purpose; the daily drip of water was measured, the growth of the stalagmite in six years was ascertained by observation, and the proportion of solid matter in the water being known, it was calculated that the "Jockey Cap" had been 259 years in course of formation.

The reader will be glad to have some authoritative account of the processes which have contributed to the formation of the marvels of the cavern. We cannot do better than lay before him a few sentences from "Rivers and Mountains of Yorkshire," by Professor Phillips, the most distinguished of Yorkshire geologists.

"The roof and sides of the cavern are everywhere intersected by fissures which were formed in the consolidation of the stone. To these fissures, and the water which has passed down them, we owe the formation of the cave and its rich furniture of stalactites. The direction of the most marked fissures is almost invariably N.W. and S.E., and when certain 'master fissures' occur, the roof of the cave is usually more elevated, the sides spread out right and left, and often ribs and pendants of brilliant stalactite placed at regular distances convert the rude fissure into a beautiful aisle of primeval architecture. Below most of the smaller fissures hang multitudes of delicate translucent tubules, each giving passage to drops of water. Splitting the rock above, these fissures admit, or formerly admitted, dropping water; continued through the floor, the larger refts permit, or formerly permitted, water to enter or flow out of the cave. By this passage of water, continued for ages on ages, the original fissure was in the first instance enlarged, through the corrosive action of streams of acidulate water. By the withdrawal of the streams to other fissures, a different process was called into operation; the fissure was bathed by drops, instead of streams of water; these drops, exposed to air currents and evaporation, yielded up the free carbonic acid to the air, and the salt of lime to the rock. Every line of drip became the axis of a stalactitical pipe from the roof; every surface bathed by thin films of liquid became a sheet of sparry deposit. The floor grew up under the droppings into fantastic heaps of stalagmite, which sometimes reaching the pipes, unite roof and floor by pillars of exquisite beauty."*

Ingleborough is the grandest of the Yorkshire mountains; although exceeded in height by Micklefell and Whernside, its position and conformation give it a commanding interest. It rises to an elevation of 2,361 feet above the level of the sea.

* For a very vivid description of this cave the reader is referred to Mr. W. White's "Month in Yorkshire."

The name is variously explained: it may be the mountain of the ingle or beacon, or the mountain of the Angles,—the English.

The mountain is usually climbed from Clapham on the south side. No difficulty is encountered in the ascent. The easiest and most gradual path is from the old road between Clapham and Ingleton, about half way between the two villages, and there is a cart-road from this point to the summit. From Settle, the nearest route is by the bridle path on the right from the top of Buckhaw Brow to Feizor, through Wharfe, and by a farm-house on the fell, called Crummock.

The ascent of Ingleborough from Chapel-le-dale is one of some interest. On the way you pass a "vast plateau of huge blocks of limestone, set with a regularity as if a paviour had placed them there." The view gradually expands northwards and eastwards. The latter part of the climb is somewhat rugged and steep.*

Ingleborough has geological peculiarities which are deserving of attention. "Its conical mass," says Phillips, "is crowned by a nearly flat-cap of mill-stone grit, and is founded on a vast tabular surface of time-worn limestone rocks, these in their turn supported by huge cliffs of massy and slaty silurian strata."

The summit of Ingleborough is very remarkable. It is a vast flat, nearly a mile in circumference. The joke in Craven is that there used formerly to be horse races on this singular level.

Ingleborough was a great hill fort, probably of the Britons. The line of defence was a wall constructed like some still existing in North Wales. Some horse-shoe shaped hut foundations still remain. They may be compared with those still so perfect on Yr Eifel in Carnarvonshire.

The view from the top of Ingleborough has been thus graphically described by Mr. Dobson:—

"Whernside kept guard before us on the north, and allowed us no peep into the dales beyond, but over its lofty summit we saw some distant hills. To the east there was Penyghent, with the valley of the Ribble stretching southward towards Settle, and northwards to its source. To the south was a beautiful and varied landscape, our view being bounded by the broad mass of Pendle, whose summit is so prominent an

* For an interesting account of an ascent of Ingleborough from Chapel-le-dale, see Mr. Wm. Dobson's " Rambles by the Ribble."

object from the greatest part of the Ribble valley; and the more humble peak of Longridge. To the west there was a beautiful extent of country stretching towards Morcambe, whose expansive sands, covered with the high tide, were broken by Warton Crag and Arnside Knott. In the distance Peel Castle can often be seen. Nearer us the Crook of Lune could be traced in the windings of that beautiful river, whose stream, like a blue streak in the landscape, was visible; and Hornby Castle appeared a picturesque spot on its proud eminence. A cloud hid from us John O'Gaunt's old castle at Lancaster. The Furness Fells were spread before us in their picturesque grouping, as well as some others of the lake mountains. We could not discern the estuary of the Ribble, though it is often seen from the top; indeed, at times the mouths of the Mersey and the Dee are discernible, whilst the glass discloses the peaks of the Isle of Man."

Mr. Dobson adds some particulars as to the botanical wealth of Ingleborough.

CHAPTER VIII.

Ingleton, Chapel-le-Dale, and Kingsdale.

Inns:—At Ingleton, Ingleborough Hotel; at Chapel-le-dale, the Hill House; at Ribble Head, Gearstones Inn.

WE started from Ingleton early in the morning, for a long day's work lay before us. In this picturesque village meet the two rivers, Doe and Greta, the former, often called the Thornton Beck, flowing down from Kingsdale. The view from Ingleton church-yard is very pretty. The ground is strangely broken up, and the houses of the village are dotted about the hill-side. There is a cotton mill close by the "meeting of waters," and further down, a handsome viaduct, by which the railway to Kirkby Lonsdale crosses the valley. A deaf old man let us into the church, and told us that he had a "awp nny" a day for winding the church clock, which made, as he calculated, a yearly salary of 15s. 2½d. Beyond this information his powers of speech seemed unable to go further than a groan of "Ay," in answer to every remark. The church having been rebuilt in 1743, "at the charge of the inhabitants," has a very plain and very modern look about it,—except the arches and pillars within, and the tower. Antiquarians, however, would be charmed with the old Norman font, which for a long time was unused and neglected, but which is really very interesting, with its interlaced round arched arcading, and its twelve carved figures, including "Christ riding upon an ass."

There was formerly no tolerable hotel at Ingleton, but four or five years ago was opened the Ingleborough Hotel, a large handsome house.

Leaving the village and turning to the left, we were soon in the lonely valley of the Greta, where for four miles, we met no human being. Between the rocky broken moors of Ingleborough, which Gray called "that huge monster of nature," and an older writer "that huge creature of God," on the right, and the slopes of Whernside on the left, the road runs parallel with the Greta, through a scene of desolation indeed. If it struck us as such on a bright August morning, what must be the impression it creates in the twilight of a drear December afternoon? Passing the mountain torrents which came down the slopes crowned by the craggy escarpments of limestone, we proceeded up the valley, which seems given up to the innumerable lapwings, whose pitiable cry appears to harmonise with the wild solitude of the dale.

At length we reached what seemed to be the source of the river, in a little hollow in the valley below the road. Crags stained with lichen rise above the source, and the bright grassy banks contrast pleasingly with the rocks. But the fact is, this is no source. The Greta has only been playing the pranks common to these rivers in the limestone; tired, as it were of daylight, it takes a plunge into the darkness beneath, and, after a subterranean course, reappears in full flow, and with a swift current, on the surface of the earth! However. it is a lovely and romantic spot. From this point the scenery becomes less wild, and a few ash trees, thorns, and hazels adorn the valley. But there is no Greta; only a dry torrent bed.

We now reached the prettily situated hamlet of Chapel-le-Dale. The tiny church, which has been immortalized by Southey in his "Doctor," is the only place of worship within many a mile—in fact between Ingleton and Hawes, and the congregation—the clergyman told us—consists of people who come from a distance, some of them as far as six miles. The little flaxen haired maiden of eight, who showed us the church, very touchingly pointed to a little grave, saying, "That's my brother's!" Entering the church, we found that it had been restored and re-pewed in 1869; it has some modern painted windows, with memorial brasses.

The reader will be pleased to peruse, in this place, Southey's charming description of this secluded spot.

"The little church, called Chapel-le-Dale, stands about a bow-shot from the family house. There they had all been carried to the font; there they had each led his bride to the altar; and there they had, each in his turn, been borne upon the shoulders of their friends and neighbours. Earth to earth they had been consigned there for so many generations, that half of the soil of the church-yard consisted of their remains. A hermit who might wish his grave to be as quiet as his cell, could imagine no fitter resting place. On three sides was an irregular low stone wall, rather to mark the limits of the sacred ground, than to enclose it; on the fourth it was bounded by the brook whose waters proceed, by a subterranean channel from Weathercote Cave. Two or three alders and rowan trees hung over the brook, and shed their leaves and seeds into the stream. Some bushy hazels grew at intervals along the lines of the wall; and a few ash trees as the winds had sown them. To the east and west some fields adjoin it in that state of half-cultivation which gives a human character to solitude: to the south, on the other side of the brook, the common, with its limestone rocks peering everywhere above the ground, extended to the foot of Ingleborough. A craggy hill, feathered with birch, sheltered it from the north.

The turf was as soft and fine as that of the adjoining hills; it was seldom broken so scanty was the population to which it was appropriated; scarcely a thistle or a nettle deformed it, and the few tomb-stones which had been placed there, were now themselves half-buried. The sheep came over the wall when they listed, and sometimes took shelter in the porch from the storm. Their voices and the cry of the kite wheeling above were the only sounds that were heard there, except when the single bell which hung in it niche over the entrance tinkled for service on the Sabbath day. or with a slower tongue gave notice that one of the child en of the soil was returning to the earth from which he sprung."

The great sight of the place is Weathercote, to see which the visitor must turn in at a gate on the left hand side of the road, and apply at Mr. Metcalfe's house for admission, for which a shilling is charged to each visitor. The reader of Mr. Boyd Dawkins' book on "Cave Hunting." will remember the interesting diagram given to show how the Greta, or Dalebeck (as he calls it) pursues an underground course in the clefts of the limestone, and how it is fed by the water which flows down Weathercote, and reveals its presence at Jingle Pot, and again at Hurtle Pot.

A door admits to a little grove from which a flight of rough hewn steps leads down to the cave. You pass under a spacious natural arch, and emerge into a vast cave open to the sky. The air of the cave is filled with spray; and this seems natural enough when you look before you. A glorious waterfall, coming from the recesses of the limestone, plunges into the abyss below. It is a grand and memorable scene. Rocks tower above—before—on each side. The precipitous cliffs are clothed with moss, and sparkle with myriads of spray drops. As the sun shines out a lovely rainbow spans the cave; and on such a forenoon as we saw it, comes and goes with sunshine and cloud. But we wished to have a nearer view of the cascade, and scrambled down, amidst loose masses and fragments of rock, into the hollow beneath. Crags overhang your head; the everlasting boom of the waterfall possesses your hearing; the air is filled with spray; the rainbow changes its form as you alter your position. Look up! Ferns and grasses wave on the heights above; the sycamores meet over the chasm to whose depths you have descended; the patch of blue sky discernible above the cave is flecked by clouds. And now we rushed behind the fall, but only to retreat, for a few seconds will suffice to drench the adventurer to the very skin.

Jingle Pot is dry and uninteresting; but Hurtle Pot is well worth seeing. It is a vast circular opening in the earth, with sycamores and beeches meeting overhead. By an opening to the south the descent is practicable down a bank of sand. At the bottom we found a deep, rocky-bedded pool. The play of sunlight penetrating the trees above gleamed upon the water, and created a tremulous light upon the rocky side. We peered into the cavern containing the water: nothing but deepness, darkness, and drip! The scene must be awsome on a gloomy or stormy day. Needless to say, the place is haunted by a "boggart!"

We proceeded on our journey, and looking back, admired the flat summit of Ingleborough, and turning to our left saw the less memorable but even loftier Whernside. The valley opened, and we were upon a tract of moss and ling. This was Batty Moss—a spot famous in the annals of the Settle and Carlisle railway. There was the viaduct and embankment which tested so severely the resources of the engineers, and which is a lasting monument of their science and perseverance. On our way through the navvy town, whose wooden walls and felt-tarred roofs we had often noticed from the line, we had a chat with a blacksmith who told us that a fair number of railway employés are still left at Batty Green. The houses, he said, were comfortable, and the situation healthy, but it was lonely, and "hard to leave," and there was no place of worship now, and no school for the children nearer than Chapel-le-Dale.

KINGSDALE.

The westerly of the two valleys which meet at Ingleton is Kingsdale, which is threaded by the river Doe. This is a desolate valley enclosed between the mountains of Graygarth and Breadagarth.

You may explore this dale either from Ingleton, or from the upper part of Chapel-le-dale; in which latter case you should visit Gatekirk Cave on the way, and proceed westward across the moors, and so in three miles strike the upper part of Kingsdale.

Thornton village—or rather the church and inn, are only a mile from Ingleton. The Force is some distance eastwards. There are two small falls and a large one, "over a high wall of limestone, lying horizontally on the vertical slate strata, out of fissures of which are growing the ash, the elm, the yew, the hazel, the holly, and the thorn. The stream, ere it takes its final leap, drops in murmuring tones from step to step in its rocky bed above, and then, with spray and roar, dashes on the projecting slate to gain a more tranquil course in the deep fosse below." The rocks on the left rise to a height of 90 feet. Access to a rocky seat behind the falls may be gained by following a path which crosses a tiny stream to the left of the fall.

If the tourist be young and nimble he may follow the river Greta upwards from Ingleton to the falls, and he will be rewarded with some beautiful bits of romantic river scenery. He must not, however, fancy he has reached Thornton Force when he comes to the first waterfalls. After an inspection of these he had better climb to the high bank on the left, and keeping to the footpath, in about half a mile the glorious sight of Thornton Force, — by some considered the finest waterfall in the district—will fill him with wonder and delight.

A fine pile of rocks above the falls, named Ravenwray, rise 50 or 60 feet on each side of the river; they have some resemblance to a lofty bridge with its arches washed away.

Four and a half miles north of Ingleton, is Yordas Cave, so named after a traditional giant, whose chamber and oven are pointed out. There are two chambers: the first 90 yards long by more than 20 high; the second circular, and tapering 50 feet to its pointed roof. In the second apartment is a cascade. In wet weather this cave is flooded, and traces of these occasional deluges are very evident.

Yordas Cave abounds in stalactites and stalagmites, many of most curious forms. As is usually the case, these singular productions of nature have been named after the objects they are supposed to resemble. To view Yordas Cave, an appointment must be made with Mrs. Whittingdale, of Westhouse, Bentham, who furnishes a guide.

An exploration of the rocky bed of the river Greta, commencing at the old slate quarries on the north-east side of the Storrs, near Ingleton, will well repay the tourist for his trouble, as here may be seen some of the wildest sights of this romantic district. For an account of this expedition, and the many other curious caves and rocks in this neighbourhood, we would refer our readers to Mr. Carr's capital little book, "Rambles about Ingleton," which may be purchased in the village.

Whernside should be ascended from the east or south east, as it is precipitous and difficult on the western side towards Dentdale. The summit commands views which are fine and extensive, but on the whole inferior to those from Ingleborough. There are three tarns near the summit of the mountain.

Weathercote.

CHAPTER IX.

The Lower Ribblesdale.

THE scenery in south-west Craven, that is, so much of the valley of the Ribble below Long Preston, as is in the county of Yorkshire, is very different from the rest of the district. Instead of mountains, scars, and torrents, we have here a pretty river-course and valley, with bordering pastures and fertile lands, adorned by several gentlemen's seats surrounded by extensive parks. The scenery is no longer wild and romantic; but it is very pleasing, and there are sites and mansions of much antiquarian and historical interest.

The Skipton and Colne railway will not be found of much use in exploring this country. The traveller from Lancashire will do well to enter Craven by Clitheroe, and take Sawley, Bolton and Gisburne, on his way to Skipton. But we will presume the tourist to be at Skipton, and to start for a long day's excursion to end at Settle. In this case, he should hire a trap and be driven as far as Gisburne, and walk the rest of the way. Better still, to give two days to the excursion and sleep at Gisburne.

The first place on the road is Broughton, near which is Broughton Hall, which has been for four centuries the home of the Tempests—one of the oldest families in Craven. The church, like that at Kirkby Malham, has niches for statues on the west sides of the columns.

East and West Marton are next passed. Marton Hall was the residence of the ancient family of the Hebers. Gledstone Hall stands on high ground and commands fine views.

Between Marton and Gisburne the tourist may take a road to the left and visit Bracewell and Barnoldswick. At Bracewell are ruins of two halls, the older one of stone, the more modern one a brick building of the time of Henry VIII. This was the ancient home of the elder branch of the family of Tempest.

Barnoldswick is chiefly noticeable as having been the first site occupied by the Cistercian monks from Fountains, who removed to Kirkstall. Henry de Lacy began to build a monastery here in 1147; but the ravages of the Scottish marauders, and the unkindly climate, seem to have disgusted the monks, for, after six years only, they forsook the place for the more secure and fertile site in the valley of the Aire.

Gisburne (Inns: Ribblesdale Arms, New Inn) is a neat little town on the east bank of the Ribble, about twelve miles from Skipton. It has a well-frequented cattle market. The church has some stained glass, and some monuments to the first and second Lords Ribblesdale, and to Sir John Assheton. Gisburne Park, at the confluence of the Ribble and Stockbeck, is famous for having, until lately, grazed a herd of wild cattle, which were probably descendents of those that ranged the forests of North Lancashire and the West Riding. They were of pure white colour, except the tip of the nose, the ears, and the feet, and were without horns. They gradually diminished in number, and the last survivors were killed off in 1859. The hall contains some good pictures. There is also a curious old drinking horn,—" a buffalo horn nearly 20 inches long, and containing about two quarts; it is supported on three silver feet resembling those of a man in armour. Round the middle is a filleting inscribed, 'QUI PUGNAT CONTRA TRES PERDET DUOS,' a seasonable though rather inconsistent warning to those who are invited to drink of it." (*Whitaker*). "Who tackles this three-legged horn will lose the use of the two legs he stands on,"—likely enough, considering the capacity of the vessel and the frailty of man!

In the Park, on the high bank of the Ribble, are the remains of a small square fort, called Castle Hough, and near it an ancient barrow.

Gisburne has been for several centuries the home of the family of Lister, by whose head and representative, Lord Ribblesdale, the place is still possessed.

Between Gisburne and Bolton the banks of the Ribble are very beautiful. Part of their beauty is owing to the abundance of timber, of which very much was planted by the first Lord Ribblesdale.

At a bend in the river is Denham Wheel, where the water whirls round with some velocity.

Three and a half miles from Gisburne, and about the same distance from Clitheroe in Lancashire, are the ruins of Sawley, or Salley Abbey. The remains are scanty; and many of the sculptured stones, once forming part of the abbey, may be seen built into the houses of the village, into the walls of the mill at Gisburne, and elsewhere; for the ruins seem to have been used as a common public quarry. They may be recognised by the armorial bearings of the great families of the district,—Percys, Tempests, Lacys, Hamertons, &c.

The monastery was founded by William de Percy, in 1147, and was colonized from Newminster, an off-shoot of Fountains. The Cistercian brotherhood seem to have been given to complaining, and apparently not without reason, both of damages sustained by the incursions of the Scots, and of the ungenial climate in which their lot was cast. They were also given to quarrelling with the monks of the neighbouring Abbey of Whalley in Lancashire. The last abbot of Sawley, William de Trafford, took part in the "Pilgrimage of Grace," and was hanged at Lancaster for that crime; as was his brother abbot of Whalley, two days after, at his own place. Upon the suppression of the foundation, Sawley was granted to Sir Arthur Darcy; it is now the property of Earl de Grey.

Recent excavations have brought to light the whole ground plan of the monastic buildings, which previously were very imperfectly traceable. The dimensions of the abbey church are very unusual. The length of the church is 185 feet, of which the nave is only 40 feet, while the choir occupies 116 feet. The transepts measure from end to end 125 feet. The transept has three eastern chapels in each wing.

There have been discovered some interesting fragments of tessellated pavement, and several monumental slabs. Here were buried Sir Robert de Clyderhow, Parson of Wigan, and Sir William de Rimington, Prior of Sawley and, in 1372, Chancellor of the University of Oxford.

Two miles from Sawley, and higher up the Ribble, is the very pleasant village of Bolton-by-Bowland,—so called to distinguish it from the other Boltons in the county. The village has a green, and on it is a stone cross. Bolton church is interesting chiefly for the monuments it contains,—to the Pudsays and their descendants, the Dawsons and Littledales. One monument is believed to be that of Sir Ralph Pudsay:

he is represented in relief with his three wives and twenty-five children! There is a handsome octagon font of grey marble, with armorial bearings of Pudsays and allied families.

Bolton Park is undulating and well timbered; and the hall is superbly situated. This is deemed the most ancient mansion in Craven; the banqueting hall dates from the time of Edward III. With Bolton Hall are associated memories of the unfortunate Sixth Henry, who was sheltered here by the devoted Lancastrian, Sir Ralph Pudsay, after the final defeat of his party at Hexham. Here, and at Whalley Abbey, Bracewell, and Waddington Hall, the crownless king was concealed for a year: he was betrayed and apprehended at the last named house, whence he was taken to the Tower. Until lately, some interesting relics of Henry's visit remained at Bolton,---a pair of boots, a pair of gloves, and a spoon, all of which were used by him during his stay here. When the property changed hands, these things were removed. A spring in the garden is called King Henry's Well; it is said to have been used by the fugitive as a bath.

Near the hall is a fine scar or cliff, overlooking the Ribble, which commands a romantically beautiful view. This is known as Rainsber Scar, or Pudsay's Leap. The latter name it acquired, according to tradition, from a remarkable incident in the history of the family of the Pudsays. Those who wish to believe the legend had better not visit the spot! This, however, is the story:—

It is said that, in the reign of Queen Elizabeth, a Pudsay of Bolton, having found silver in a field at Rimington, infringed the royal prerogative and coined shillings.

> "Oh, then he made, and thought no ill,
> The Pudsay shillings his debts to pay,—
> Still at the Mint, by Bolton Mill,
> The dross of his works is seen to-day."

For this offence, "brave Pudsay, he was doomed to dee." Pressed by the soldiers, he flung himself on his horse's back, and galloped straight to Rainsber Scaur.

> "Now for a leap, quoth brave Pudsay!
> If of death I must meet the shock,
>   Since it may no other be;
> Better a leap from my own good rock,
>   Than from a ladder at York, quoth he!
> Into his steed he drove the spur,—
>   Fearfully he did snort and neigh;
> Yet, though at first he was hard to stir,
>   Over the Scaur leaped Wanton Grey!"

The culprit rode hard, until he came into the presence of the Queen, his god-mother, who was upon a ship in the Thames. The interview and its result must be related in the racy vernacular:—

"An a fell upoo his knees, an a sed, 'Pardon, Pardon!'
An shu sed, 'Wat ivver has ta bin abeout, Poodsaa?'
An a sed, 'Pardon! Pardon!'
An thir wir a deal spak for him, and sed a wir a reet gentlemon, an it didn't look loike at a sud do eouet wrang.
An shu sed, 'Weel, then, eouet, Coozn Poodsaa, but moordir.'
An a sed it wir nobbut coinin.
An shu sed, 'Waugh!' But she teld him at a moodn't mak ony moar a thir Poodsaa shillings.
An a didn't."

In the woods, half a mile above the Scar, is a cave of considerable proportions.

The tourist who wishes to explore the uttermost south-western corner of Craven may continue his journey, by Waddington Hall and Bashall, to Mitton, where the Hodder joins the Ribble; and may visit Browsholme Hall, an old Henry VII. house, in the valley of the Hodder. In Mitton church is a beautiful group of sepulchral statues and monuments of the Sherburne family.

The forest of Bowland or Bolland occupies the hilly region on the west of the river Hodder. The village of Slaidburn is on its eastern edge, in the valley.

From Gisburne or Bolton the tourist may proceed to Settle, either by the valley of the Ribble, or by a somewhat more direct road to the east. In the former case he will pass Paythorn, where is a bridge over the river, Nappa, where are some islands in the centre of the stream, and Halton, near which is Halton Place, a house occupying a commanding position; and so by Long Preston to Settle. The other route is by Forest Becks, Wigglesworth, and Rathmell.

CHAPTER X.

THE SETTLE AND CARLISLE RAILWAY.

OF all modes of travelling on wheels, there is one preeminent in luxurious comfort. Need we say that we refer to a journey in a Pullman Car on a Midland express? Availing ourselves of this latest product of refined civilization, we took our places in the palace car which is attached to the Scotch express, on a bright and breezy day at the end of July. We were bound for the Craven country, and for the wild moorland, mountainous region which has just been opened up to travellers and tourists by the new line from Settle to Carlisle. Seated on crimson velvet-piled arm chairs, which, being fixed upon a pivot, admit of a semi-revolution, and surrounded by maps, guides, and time-tables, we prepared to enjoy the varied scenery through which we were to be driven by a powerful engine at a high speed, and yet with the utmost possible ease and comfort. As a conductor had said at the outset of the journey to a gentleman at St. Pancras, who was debating with himself whether he should travel to Scotland in the Pullman, "You save your seven shillings in wear and tear; at the end of the journey, instead of feeling cramped, and worn and weary, if not half shaken to pieces, you will feel as if you had been resting in your own drawing room." The gentleman took the advice, and seemed pleased with the bargain. Certainly it is no small advantage to have what may be called a series of French windows on both sides of the carriage, not only admitting abundance of light, but enabling you to see the country on either hand as well as the rapid pace permits.

Punctually at the hour we were at Normanton, where half-an-hour is allowed to dine. We have always eschewed railway refreshment rooms, and needed some persuasion to induce us to give the dinner a trial. However, we can testify that the arrangements are wonderfully different from those of any other such place we have entered, that is, in this country. The dining room was only temporary, but was very comfortable. No sooner are you seated than the soup is before you, and the fish is ready before you are, and is followed by *entrée* and joint, and these by sweets and cheese. Neat handed Phyllis sees that no time is lost in changing plates. Your bottle of Burgundy or hock stands before you, with the price ticket hung round its neck, and if you give the word, the cork is drawn *instanter*. You have your clear half-hour for the meal, and we venture to say pay your three shillings and sixpence with a better grace than you ever displayed at the refreshment counter at Mugby Junction. Returning to the car, and retiring to a cosy smoking-room to enjoy a post-prandial cigar, we resumed our interest in the route.

Leaving Leeds on our right—for the Leeds passengers had changed carriages at Normanton, that they might not be delayed by our dinner, and that we might not be delayed by entering Leeds station—we dashed past the romantic ruins of Kirkstall, and soon found ourselves in the seclusion of verdant Airedale. Farewell, for some weeks let us hope, to the chimneys and the smoke of thronged and busy cities! Away to the clearer atmosphere, the brighter skies, the keener air of mountains. Away past the smiling cornfields, and the bright green meadows where the last hay-cocks wait to be carried to the stacks; away, past the meek, meditative kine, the startled colt, the flustered sheep. Away, between the broad grassy slopes and hill sides, streaked by the grey stone walls of Yorkshire, where the ash trees are ruffled by the west wind; past the rivulets hurrying down the rocky bed, and gleaming in the summer sun; past the dingle clad with bracken, where the proud foxglove rears its stately head. Away, towards the mossy moors, where the rivers have their rise, to the mountain peaks that lord it over the undulating landscapes of the north!

At Skipton we had to leave our express and join a stopping train, for our friend, the Scotchman was not to pause between Skipton and Carlisle.

But let us, before recounting our experiences, and recording our observations, give the reader a general idea of the country to be traversed, and some notion of the magnitude and difficulty of the undertaking which the Midland Company has so successfully accomplished. The Pennine Chain is the great mountain range which divides the North of England longitudinally into two unequal parts. It extends from the Scottish border southwards into Derbyshire. In north-west Yorkshire and in Westmoreland this Pennine Chain rears its loftiest summits. Ingleborough rises to a height of 2373 feet, Pennegent to 2231 feet feet, and Whernside to 2414 feet. And these are only the best known of a multitude of stupendous fells and pikes, which render this district, with the adjoining lake country, the most mountainous in England. As the local rhymes run :—

> "Pendle, Pennegent, and Ingleborough,
> You'll find no higher hills if you march all England thorough."

or according to another version :—

> "Ingleborough, Pendle Hill, and Pennegent,
> Are the highest hills between Scotland and Trent."

These lines embody a popular error; for Micklefell is nearly 2600 feet high.

Now the reader will remember that, until lately, there have been two routes to Scotland, the east and west coast routes, by Newcastle and Berwick, and by Lancaster and Carlisle respectively. It was natural enough that the Midland Company, having secured a road to Lancaster and Morcambe by the Airedale valley and Ribblesdale, and having taken possession of north-western Yorkshire, should turn a longing eye northwards, and set its heart upon establishing communications with North Britain, and gaining a share of the through Scotch traffic, said to be worth two millions a year. Whoever wishes to read the several chapters of this book of modern railway history, should refer to the laborious, interesting, and handsomely got up volume of Mr. Williams, "The Midland Railway, its rise and progress." It was at length resolved that a direct line north, commencing at Settle should be constructed, at a cost exceeding two millions sterling. The result is the Midland route, as distinguished from those mentioned above, and intermediate in its course, although nearer the west coast than the east.

It was one thing to determine upon the work, and another thing to do it. The obstacles were tremendous, but engineering, like love, "will find out a way." But how was the route fixed? The country being, for upwards of 20 miles, one mass of mountain and moor, how was it to be traversed by an iron road? The will be better understood by the help of an ordnance map. But without this aid we can enable the reader to understand how the thing was done. The engineers had recourse to nature, and found that she had been doing their work for them for thousands of years beforehand, as if in preparation for what was to come, that the task might, when in due time undertaken, be an easier one for the hands of man. Natural forces had been cutting hollow channels amongst the hills, and deepening and widening rifts into valleys, and intersecting the stupendous masses with the winding waterways. Although the difficulties remaining were enormous—on the whole probably such as railway engineers have nowhere else, throughout the length and breadth of the country, been called to encounter—still these valleys were, so to speak, the fulcrum which enabled the lever of mechanical science to be brought to bear. Southwards, Ribblesdale offered an inlet into the very heart of the district. The Ribble, rising on the south-western slopes of Cam Fell, and flowing between Whernside and Ingleborough on the west, and Pennegent on the east; and lower down, between Stackhouse and Moughton on the west, and Langcliffe and Stainforth on the east, seemed to invite a road of iron to keep it company and track its course. Northwards, the valley of the Eden, as lovely as that of the Ribble is wildly romantic, furnished an accessible pathway towards Carlisle. Indeed, the chief difficulties of the road might be considered as surmounted when once the course of the Eden was reached. Between these two valleys lay the most formidable difficulties and obstacles. Availing themselves, however, of two great, but minor valleys, Dentdale and Garsdale, and tunnelling beneath some elevated moors, the engineers were able to vanquish every hindrance, and to establish a connection between Ribblesdale and the Eden valley, and thus between Settle and Carlisle.

The reader will now see what it was that brought us to Settle; we were attracted by some of the wildest country in all England, pierced by a railway which is admitted to be a triumph of engineering skill and perseverance.

At Settle we put up for the night at the Golden Lion, and next morning, after an early breakfast, prepared to make a general survey of the new line. There are three stations bearing the name of Settle; that on the old line to Clapham and Lancaster, the junction station where the lines diverge, and the new station on the new line. It was to this last named that we proceeded. We were favoured with the company of gentlemen who were familiar with every mile of the road, and who had watched its progress during the whole six years occupied in its construction.

All the stations on the line are remarkably neat and commodious; the station master's houses are like village manses, and the cottages for the porters are models of their kind. We could not but admire the pretty station at Settle. This and three neighbouring stations are built of Bradford stone, which, with dressings of the same, were brought here ready dressed, and the station buildings were accordingly easily constructed. The station masters' houses on this line, with their gables and high roofs, are models of domestic architecture; of their occupants we may say (though in some cases this holds good rather of the dwellings than of the localities), "the lines have fallen to them in pleasant places." The bright-hued flowers bloom in the neat gardens and in jars of porcelain in the windows. Within, judging by the glimpses we enjoyed, these dwellings are equally attractive. Signs of taste and of education abound; one cannot but feel that railways are giving employment to a class of men whose intelligence, abilities, and general character, are of the highest value to the public.

Our train appeared, and we took our seats, and were soon puffing away up Ribblesdale. Leaving the open pastures of Settle we found ourselves ascending a narrow valley, which we tracked, sometimes by a cutting through perpendicular strata of rock, sometimes by a handsome bridge over the rocky bed of the Ribble, sometimes by an embankment affording a view of green pastures, with their grazing sheep, and here and there a whitewashed cottage; but never, by any chance, traversing a bit of level ground. Indeed, it was drolly said, when the line was in process of construction, that between Settle and Carlisle not enough level ground could be discovered to build a house upon! It is, in truth, a wild, bare, and rugged country; and before the line was made, must have been one of the dreariest districts in all England. One cannot but feel that we live in innovating days, when drawn in a luxurious carriage at a speed of forty miles through desolations guarded by mountain barriers and peaty moors, and tenanted by the sheep of the wilderness. There is a striking contrast visible from the line in two bridges spanning the river close by. An ancient narrow bridge, mossy with age, has been superseded by one constructed to carry the road traffic of this solitude over both railway and river; and they stand side by side, works of the olden and modern times. Pennegent, with its whale-like outlines, raises its colossal mass on our right as we approach Horton, whose square towered church stands among a knot of grey and whitewashed houses. Passing through a cutting made in the boulder-clay, we come to Selside.

A few facts will be mentioned as we proceed in illustration of the engineering difficulties which were encountered and overcome in the construction of this part of the Settle and Carlisle railroad. They were communicated to us by one of the engineers employed throughout the whole period of six years and a half occupied in the works.

The cold and elevated situation of the district may be understood when it is known that the engineers proceeded northwards from Settle thirty-two miles before they came to a ploughed field, which was near Bull Ghyl, near Kirkby Stephen. Even in the southern part of the Eden valley there is a great preponderance of grass land, and much less ploughed land than formerly. The tenant of Wharton Hall mentioned to us that of the 600 acres and upwards he farmed, a very small portion was under the plough, only enough for home use. A hundred and thirty acres were meadow, and the rest pasture.

The ground itself in which the navvies had to work often presented serious difficulties. The boulder-clay is of very unequal consistency, and Mr. Williams mentioned that, in some instances, the labourer would strike his pick-axe with force into what appeared to be a soft clay, and would encounter a hard rock just below the surface; and that an experience like this would so annoy and disgust the not too sensitive navvy, that he would lay down his tools at once and leave the work. An engineer on the line remarked to us that the softer material often occasioned more trouble than the hard. Clay, when acted upon by rain, became soft mud, and in tunnelling, especially, was continually coming down and filling up the passage already made.

Near to Batty Green we enter a somewhat remarkable cutting. When travelling through it before it was finished, we noticed that the banks had slipped down nearly on to the permanent way, or the ballast. The remark was then made to the engineer, "You will find it necessary to have these banks cleared out." He told us that not only had the soil slipped, but the whole walls of the cutting had slipped down and crushed under the permanent way, so as to lift up the whole of the road. "We shall have," he said, "to take out the whole road—sleepers, rails, and all,—to deepen the cutting, and to relay the road." This, of course, was thoroughly and efficiently done, before the line was opened.

Leaving grand old Ingleborough on our left, and passing Ribblehead on our right, where the Ribble takes its rise on the slopes of Cam Fell, we come to Batty Green. Here has existed, for several years past, a town of the most extraordinary description. Some of the most difficult work upon the Settle and Carlisle line lies in this neighbourhood. And here, accordingly, out in this wild moorland wilderness, was fixed the habitation of the navvies whose strong hands were to do the great work. Some two thousand of these brawny armed sons of toil were located at Batty Green; and we passed the temporary town of wooden felt-covered huts which was erected for their accommodation. The work which these men had to do was of no ordinary kind. "Here," says Mr. Williams, "five great railway works follow one another in succession--the viaduct, the embankment, the cutting, the tunnel, and then another viaduct." Crossing a vast peaty bog by the Batty Moss Viaduct—the longest on the line and 100 feet in height—laid securely upon the most soft and apparently impossible foundation, and leaving the great moss of Whernside on our left, we approach Blea Moor tunnel. Our readers may have noticed, that when the presentation of his portrait to Mr. Allport, the manager of the Midland Railway, was made a short time ago at Derby, allusion was made to the circumstance that, at Mr. Allport's suggestion, the "distance" of the picture consisted of a view of Blea Moor. In fact, this was looked upon as the "crux" of the undertaking; and the vanquishing of this obstacle may justly be regarded as one of the triumphs of railway enterprise and engineering skill. The moor is 1250 feet above the level of the sea, and the tunnel is carried through at a distance of some 500 feet below the summit.

Near Blea Moor tunnel is the "summit level" of the line, being 1150 feet above the sea; yet this is reached by gradients never exceding 1 in 100.

We emerged into Dentdale, near the source of the little river Dee, which, after tracking the beautiful dale of which

Dent is the capital, falls into the Rother at Sedbergh. Passing over the romantic dingle by the Dent Head viaduct, we enjoyed a charming prospect towards the west, down the lovely vale of the Dee. Far below us the beck pursued its rapid course, hurrying in places over a black marble bed. As we gazed upon the smiling verdure of this fascinating vale abounding in homesteads nestling among the meadows, and flanked by noble hills, we could not but form purposes of exploration.

At Arten Ghyll viaduct the ground was discovered to be so insecure that it was necessary to go down 50 feet to get foundations. A shaft was made by digging down from six to ten feet; then the shaft was timbered round with strong timbers. Progress having thus been made and satisfactorily ensured, the shaft was carried a few feet farther, until the required depth was obtained. All the time that this operation was proceeding, and until a firm foundation was reached it was necessary to continue pumping out the water as it rose in the shaft.

At Rise Hill tunnel we are in another of the critical engineering points of this interesting line. Here, as we were told by the resident engineer, on account of the horizontal strata of blue limestone which constituted the roof, it was found necessary to place wrought iron ribs across the tunnel, at distances of six feet apart. These ribs were made to spring from the side walls of the tunnel, and so to form an arch, which supports it. They are fastened together with tie rods. In this manner an iron framework has been fixed in this tunnel for the space of 200 yards.

On emerging from this tunnel, we found ourselves in Garsdale, which is upon our route, the transition valley between Dentdale and the valley of the Eden. The prodigious works we had passed could scarcely be unnoticed by the most unobservant traveller; yet it requires some acquaintance with the processes of railway construction to appreciate them as they deserve. Above the very tunnel we had just left behind there had been built, we were informed, another village of huts, at an elevation of 1300 feet above the sea level, in which for several years 350 inhabitants had made their mountain homes. From here there was a tramway down a steep incline to the road in Garsdale, 600 yards in length, up which all the railway material for this portion of the line had to be drawn by a rope worked by steam power."

We soon reached a spot which is one of the landmarks of the route. This is the Moorcock Inn—a name suggestive of the nature of the locality. We noticed that, in some places, the telegraph wires were twisted into a single cable, to avoid injury to the grouse, which it was feared, might in their flight strike themselves against the wires. And we were told that, in other places, the owners of the moors, for the same reason, required that the telegraph wires should be buried below the surface of the soil. Grouse and moor-fowl seem to be the most important inhabitants of the district. At the Moorcock is the meeting of several roads—that to Hawes in Wensleydale; that to Sedbergh, by Garsdale; and that to Kirkby Stephen. Passing over the Dandry Mire Viaduct, near to which is the junction station for Hawes,—which is reached by a branch line,—we were soon at Ais Gill Moor, the summit of thr railway, at 1167 feet above the sea-level. Yet, though a height so unusual is reached, the gradients on the Settle and Carlisle line never exceed one in one hundred. And now we are in Westmoreland, in the valley of the Eden, with Wild Boar Fell upon our left and Mallerstang Edge (pronounced Mawstan) upon our right. Passing Deep Gill, "where the union of a bridge and culvert has been ingeniously designed to meet the requirements of the site, which is composed of a stream pouring a cascade off a high shelf of rock," we soon look down upon the winding course of the romantic Eden. This celebrated stream well justifies the quaint conceit of the old poet, who sang of it thus:—

"Fetched from Paradise, the honour came
Rightfully borne; for Nature gives thee flowers
That have no rivals amongst British bowers;
And thy bold rocks are worthy of their fame."

Before reaching Kirkby Stephen Station the railway train passes through Birkett Tunnel. Immediately to the south of this are the evidences of what is known to geologists as the Pennine Fault. Crossing the line at this point, the Fault may be traced in a south-westerly direction towards and across Dent Valley. We were informed by one of the engineers that in making Birkett Tunnel they found the work comparatively easy, because the displaced strata are, in that place, in a vertical position. Whereas horizontal strata present a flat roof across the top of the tunnel—which occasions great engineering difficulties—when the strata are vertical no great difficulty is experienced in working the tunnel to the exact section required—the form of the section being that of the pointed arch. Very curious and interesting is the insight which the railway cutting in this place affords into the almost perpendicular arrangement of intermingled geological strata. The traveller should not fail to observe it as he passes.

A heavy "slip" took place in the construction of Birkett Tunnel. The ground came down for the space of 60 feet in length. This part of the tunnel had to be lined throughout, and filled with wooden sleepers put across, side by side.

A hundred yards or so before entering the Fault, the traveller by the railway train should look eastward over the valley of the Eden. At this point three buildings are seen in a line; the middle one, a square tower of dark stone, standing boldly up on a green knoll, is Pendragon Castle. As the traveller approaches the Kirkby Stephen station, he may observe a tuft of trees in the valley; behind these nestle the ruins of Wharton Hall. On the hills above—the heights of Mallerstang—may be descried a lofty stone. This is one of nine erect pillars, known as the "Ninĕ Stands."

By the time we reached the station of Kirkby Stephen, the day had brightened, and sunshine and breeze contributed to the enjoyment of our excursion. There is no doubt that the district is a very rainy one. The rain gauge showed that during 1872 ninety-two inches of rain fell at Dent Head. The extreme rainfall of the region interfered very materially with the progress of the contractors' works upon the line, both by its influence upon the soil, ãnd by its limiting the number of working days to an unusual extent. The same phenomenon accounts, however, for the singular greenness of these moorlands, and especially of the valleys which they enclose. Speaking of weather, we may remark that there were many days during the construction of the Settle and Carlisle railway, when the winds were so violent, that in certain exposed positions upon the line, it was utterly impossible for the workmen to proceed with their task. On the embankments and bridges they would have been literally blown away. We were thankful for a very different day for our explorations by the banks of the Eden.

Smardale Viaduct is a great work which occupied four and a half years in the construction. It is over Scandal Beck and the South Durham Railway, and is 130 feet in height from stream to rail. It contains more than 60,000 tons of stone.

Other viaducts, tunnels, cuttings, and embankments followed, too numerous to mention; a list of them will be found at the end of this chaper.

After leaving Kirkby Stephen behind us, we found the scenery much less wild. While in many parts of England the grass had been well-nigh scorched up, here we observed it bright with verdure. There were a few green crops; the hedgerows were a pleasing variety after so many stone walls as we had remarked in the more elevated country. Passing Crosby Garrett and Ormside, our eyes were refreshed by the ripening cornfields, whilst here and there the red sandstone rocks offered a picturesque diversity in the landscape. After a journey of 42 miles from Settle, we reached Appleby, the quiet little capital of Westmoreland. One of the railway officials characterized the pretty, but by no means go-a-head little town, in a few words, thus: "Appleby, sir, has been asleep for a few hundred years, but, now the railway has come here, it is beginning to rub its eyes, and may perhaps soon wake up." According to the historian of Westmoreland everything belonging to Appleby—the town, the corporation, the assizes, the market—has existed from time immemorial. And we are disposed to receive this historian's opinion with profound respect, because of his wholesome scepticism regarding Julius Cæsar's Tower, as it is called, a portion of Appleby Castle. Says Mr. Sayers of this famous keep—which, by the bye, is clearly seen from the railway—"Popular tradition says that it was raised by Julius Cæsar; however, we think its erection might with equal propriety be attributed to Napoleon Buonaparte!"

Passing Battle Barrow bank, where was another navvy-town of huts, we reached Long Marton, the station of which has, instead of a wall, a fence of iron rails, with wire-work filling it in. Asking the reason of this, we were told that this arrangement was for the purpose of affording a picturesque view of and from the station, and that the net-work was to prevent children straying or falling through! We admit that the reader can scarcely be expected to believe this explanation: fancy a railway with æsthetic susceptibilities!

And now, on our left, upon the western horizon we discerned the romantic forms of the Lake Mountains about Keswick. Passing Newbiggin and the pretty Crowdundle Beck we approached the confluence of the Eamont with the Eden; the former river comes down from Ullswater. On the west might be observed, among noble woods, the roofs of Eden Hall, the home of the Musgroves. An old manuscript says of this famous place:—"Walks as fine as Chelsea fields, the fair Eden gliding like the Thames along!" Our readers will be familiar with the tradition concerning the "Luck of Edenhall." "A servant of the family going to fetch water from the well, saw the fairies dancing round this vessel. He snatched it from them, and they entreated him to restore it; but on his refusal, they uttered the ominous words—

'Whene'er this cup shall break or fall,
Farewell the luck of Edenhall."

The "luck" is a curious old vessel of green-coloured glass, ornamented with foliage, and enamelled in different colours.

The scenery about Longwathby is extemely romantic. Far away on the east rises the grand mountain mass known as Cross Fell. Westward you look over the winding Eden, where groups of quiet cattle stand cooling their feet in the sparkling shallows, towards the woods which form a picturesque horizon to the landscape. Near Little Salkeld, on the summit of a hill, will be found the Druidical remains, known as Long Meg and her Daughters,—"that family forlorn," as Wordsworth has finely termed them.

And now we come to Lazonby—the goal of our present railway journey. Prettily is the station situated; among fir trees, fruit orchards, and sunny farmsteads, with the church and churchyard on a pleasant knoll, looking over the charming vale below.

Near Lazonby is the seat of Colonel Maclane, who is said to have predicted the construction of a railway between Settle and Carlisle 30 years before that work was undertaken!

At Eden Brow the "tipping" went on for two years. As the work proceeded, the material tipped merely slipped down, carrying trees with it in its course, and depositing them in the adjoining country.

There is very romantic scenery bordering the line all the way between Lazonby and Armathwaite Stations; and, though not so fine, yet pretty scenery between Armathwaite and Cote Hill. The river Eden here flows through a deep dingle, clad on both sides in places, with umbrageous trees from the bank of the river to the summits of the hills. This country must be visited, either from Carlisle on the north, or from the plain village inn of Kirkoswald on the south. It may be questioned whether more beautiful scenery is to be found in all England than in this valley of the Eden.

Carlisle is a busy station, both for passenger and for goods traffic. Seven railway companies run their lines into this one station.

NOTE TO CHAPTER X.

The following list of the Viaducts and Tunnels which have been constructed on the new railway, will give the reader some notion of the magnitude and difficulty of the engineering work which has been accomplished. The dimensions and other particulars are annexed according to the official statements.

LIST OF VIADUCTS.

No.	Name of Viaduct.	No. of Arches.	Length in ft.	Height in feet at deepest part	Span of Arches in ft.
1	Settle, Kirkgate	4	130	22	30
2	Settle, Giggleswick Road	6	269	35	5 of 30 and 1 of 40
3	Batty Moss	24	1328	100	45
4	Dent Head	10	596	100	45
5	Arten Gill	11	645	100	45
6	Dandry Mire	12	700	50	45
7	Quarry	4	270	54	45
8	Ais Gill	4	270	65	45
9	Smardale	12	700	130	45
10	Crosby Garrett	6	270	53	38
11	High Grisbrow	6	370	70	45
12	River Eden	10	590	84	45
13	Troutbeck	5	319	55	45
14	Crowdundle Beck	4	270	50	45
15	Briggle Beck	7	420	50	45
16	River Eden	7	421	55	45
17	Armathwaite	9	530	80	45
18	Dry Beck	6	370	80	45
19	High Stand Gill	4	270	60	45

LIST OF TUNNELS.

No.	Name of Tunnel	Length in Yards.	Depth in feet.	Strata.
1	Taitlands	120	40	Blue Limestone
2	Blea Moor	2640	500	Gritstone, Limestone & Shale
3	Rise Hill	1180	180	Blue Limestone
4	Moor Cock	100	64	Boulder Clay
5	Quarry	70	50	Boulder Clay
6	Birkett	428	100	Limestone
7	Crosby Garrett	180	66	Gritstone, Limestone & Flint
8	Helm	500	110	Red Marl
9	Culgaith	650	110	Red Marl
10	Lazonby	100	110	Red Sandstone
11	Baron Woods	200	90	Red Sandstone
12	Baron Woods	250	80	Red Sandstone
13	Armathwaite	320	84	Red Sandstone

CHAPTER XI.

UPPER RIBBLESDALE, DENT HEAD, AND HAWES.

IN this chapter we will briefly describe four excursions from so many successive stations upon the Settle and Carlisle Railway.

1. *From Horton Station.* At Horton-in-Ribblesdale are two inns, either of which will afford comfortable quarters for the pedestrian. The New Inn is by the bridge, and the Lion Inn is by the church. The church has arches and columns of the Norman period, and a font equally ancient; the tower dates from Henry VII. or VIII. The grammar-school is well endowed; the present building replaces one which stood in the churchyard.

From Horton the summit of Pennegent (or Penyghent) may most easily be climbed. The ascent of the mountain, which is a mass of limestone capped with millstone grit, and 2273 feet high, is very easy. The direct path is up the Greenrake, a broad grassy track between two projecting rocks. " The early morning," says Mr. Howson, "the noon, and the evening have each their peculiar advantages for the ascent of such mountains as Pennegent and Ingleborough. Soon after sunrise, when the clouds are dispersing and beginning to assume a higher altitude, their slow and solemn motion, the haze in the valleys, the illumined summit of the hills, like pleasant islands in these lakes of mists, the grand pictorial effects of light and shade, and the purity and freshness of the air, may well tempt the tourist to select such an hour. In the evening, too, the pageantry of a sunset may have its peculiar charms; but, as the chief object in ascending a mountain is to obtain an extensive view of the surrounding country, the noon, unless there has been a succession of dry and hot days, will be found to be the most eligible time for such a purpose."

Following the course of the stream which joins the Ribble at Horton, the visitor will come to Doukgill Scar, an amphitheatre of rock, with beetling brow, threatening to fall upon the spectator below. The rock is over-grown with moss and ferns, and is crowned with a plantation of larch.

Not far from the cart-track to the summit of Pennegent are some of those singular caverns, locally known as "pots," which are so characteristic of the mountain limestone. The most remarkable of these are Thirl Pot and Thund Pot, which are both well worth a visit. Each is a terrific chasm, and the receptacle of a mountain torrent. They are somewhat dangerous to approach. Thund Pot has been plumbed to a depth of 200 feet.

Distances from Horton:—To Clapham, 6 miles; Ingleton, by Clapham, 10 miles; Ingleton, by Selside, 8 miles; Litton, 7 miles; Settle, 6 miles.

2. *From Ribblehead.* From hence is to be made one of the most marvellous of all the Ribblesdale excursions. No visitor should lose the opportunity of seeing Helln Pot, which is to be found from the hamlet of Selside, by following first a green lane, then a brook, and then looking for a solitary bush-like tree as a landmark. This Helln Pot is the most awful thing in all England. It is a terrific chasm 180 feet in length, and 60 in width, but 200 deep and more! It is walled round by a high wall, for the protection of cattle, and indeed of all living things unwinged; but it may be crossed by a wooden bridge, placed there by recent explorers. Trees partially overshadow the yawning abyss; as you look down, not without a shudder, you remark ledges of rock clothed with moss and grass, and below, at one side, a waterfall, which plunges into the depth. Several attempts have been made to explore this chasm; the last, the only thoroughly successful one, in 1870, by an adventurous party of thirteen, including three ladies! Mr. Birkbeck was the conductor, and Mr. Boyd Dawkins, who tells the story in his "Cave Hunting," was one of the explorers. Provided with suitable apparatus, and aided by a party of navvies, the enthusiasts were rewarded for their enterprise by very interesting observations and discoveries. Some of them reached a depth of 300 feet from the surface—having descended in the darkness, through the courses of several waterfalls. They were five hours about the business.

There are two other caves above, by which the sides of Helln Pot may be reached. Looking into them we were struck by the flatness of the roofs, the honeycombed limestone walls, the perpetual murmur of invisible water. To explore them, a visitor must be suitably provided with lights and ladders, and be prepared for a wetting.

From Ribbblehead Station, proceeding westwards, the tourist may visit Chapel-le-dale, or climb Ingleborough. But this excursion has been described in Chapter VIII. Turning eastwards, however, you will, in a mile and a half, reach the inn at Gearstones, a roomy and comfortable hostelry in a wild, secluded spot upon the high road from Hawes to Ingleton.

After luncheon in the inn at Gearstones, you may set off to see Thorns Gill, a deep cleft in the limestone, with steep cliffs overhung with ash and rowan, through which flows the stream, Gale Beck, which is the chief confluent of the Ribble —though not that coming from Ribblehead, as it is called, close by Gearstones. The channel is remarkably tortuous, and is diversified, here with a deep, dark pool, and there with the small pot holes peculiar to the district. These pot-holes are bored by stones, which are whirled round and round by by the eddying of the streams. The beck is crossed by a plank-bridge, and lower down by an arch of stone.

Adjoining Thorns Gill is a cave, called Catknot Hole, which has been robbed of the stalactites that were formerly its glory.

From Gearstones or Horton the tourist should not fail to visit Lynn Gill, a wild and romantic mountain ravine, through which flows the Cam Beck, another confluent of the Ribble. On the road between Lynn Gill and Horton, near a farmhouse called Old Ing, is Brow Gill, a cavern with an imposing entrance, and near New Houses, one mile from Horton, are two chasms worth looking at, Jackdaw Hole and Sel Gill.

From Gearstones also may be made the ascent of Blea Moor, whence is a wide and glorious prospect; or the old, disused high road may be followed over Cam Fell to Hawes; or the road to Newby Head, where is a good country inn, and whence you can descend into Wensleydale.

Distances from Gearstones: To Chapel-le-dale, 3 miles; to Dent, 9 miles; to Hawes, 9 miles; to Sedbergh, 16 miles; to Linn Gill Bridge, 2 miles; to Horton, 6 miles.

3. *From Dent Head Station*, the tourist should explore the lovely valley of the Dent. The little river Dee runs through this valley, and rushes over a bed paved as it were with black

marble. The little town of Dent (Inns: George and Dragon;
the Sun) is eight miles down the valley. Here was born Prof.
Sedgwick, the distinguished geologist. This is the scene of
Southey's story in "The Doctor," "the terrible knitters of Dent."
The excursion may be continued to Sedbergh (Inn: King's
Arms) near which are How Gill Fells and the Calf, Black Foss,
a tremendous chasm and waterfall, and Cautley spout, a
succession of cascades, measuring altogether 860 feet. At
Sedbergh is a grammar-school (first grade classical) with a
very wealthy foundation.

5. *From Hawes Junction Station.* The tourist may follow
the Garsdale valley westwards to Sedbergh, or he may turn
eastward down the valley of the Ure, the uppermost portion
of the celebrated Wensleydale; or, he may take the branch
line to Hawes (Inn: The White Hart), the highest town in
this dale. This town is the centre for many delightful
excursions. "Seven Dales, Mossdale, Yoredale proper, Cotter-
dale, and Fossdale (north), and Widdale, Galedale, and
Seamerdale (south), open out within three miles of Hawes,
radiating from it north, south, and west." (*Murray*). Hardraw
Force is a very beautiful cascade in the neighbourhood of
Hawes.

Brow Gill.

CHAPTER XII.

THE VALLEY OF THE EDEN.

WE will ask the reader to accompany us in three excursions we made in the lovely valley of the Eden, including much of the most beautiful scenery and most interesting objects to be visited in the district. The three stations upon the line from which we started were Kirkby Stephen, Appleby, and Lazonby.

Within an easy walk from Kirkby Stephen station are three interesting remains of antiquity. Accompanied by one of the railway engineers, to whom a residence of several years and his professional duties had rendered the whole country familiar, we set out upon a little antiquarian excursion. Crossing the fields, by the courteous permission of the tenant farmer, Mr. Cleasby, we proceeded to inspect the remains of Wharton Hall. When we say "remains," it must be understood that, although the former glory of the place has departed, there is still, in good repair, enough to constitute a very commodious farm-house.

The Wharton family held this place from the reign of Edward I. down to the year 1728, when the estate was sold to Robert Lowther, Esq., ancestor of the Earls of Lonsdale. The last Duke of Wharton is remembered in history and celebrated in poetry for his brilliant abilities, his chequered career, his dissolute character, and his expatriation and early death. This nobleman was the subject of Pope's lines, commencing

"Wharton, the scorn and wonder of our days,
Whose ruling passion was the lust of praise."

Entering the paddock or enclosure, within which stands Wharton Hall, our attention was directed to the curious water-worn stone posts of the gate. These were singularly indented specimens of the "breccia" or "brockram" stone, which is found abundantly in the neighbourhood of Kirkby Stephen, and is commonly used for buildings of various kinds, for walls, &c. There are two kinds of conglomerate; the pudding stone, the imbedded pebbles of which are round, and the brockram, which abounds in pebbles of an angular form. The latter, so common here, is a calcareous, magnesian formation.

Through a grove of sycamores, elms, and ash trees, we approached the hall—a stone building, with some traces of former grandeur in its mullioned windows, its enormous chimney-places, and the coat of arms engraven over the gateway, bearing the date, 1559. Passing through this gateway under the tower, we entered the spacious quadrangle. The buildings fronting us and on our left we saw at once to be inhabited, and found them to be occupied by the household of the farmer, and by his farm servants. An immense fire-place, 12 feet across, fronted us, and looked picturesque enough, with its verdant mantling of ivy. This was the hearth where blazed of old, upon the dog irons, the logs of the dining or banqueting hall fire. On the right of this apartment is the ancient kitchen, which has been roofed at a period comparatively recent; it has two large fire-places, one of them half filled in with masonry. This room has been used as a smithy. Beneath it is a vaulted cellar, 30 feet by 15, which is considered to have been the larder, doubtless well replenished in the olden time with many a fat buck from the forest of Mallerstang, and many a salmon from the silvery waters of the Eden.

The chapel of the hall is on the left of the quadrangle, and is now used as a store-room. It is the outer side of this portion of the edifice that the visitor sees in approaching by way of the plantation. The hall of the present dwelling is reached by a flight of steps from the outside; on the right of the hall is the lord's solar, or private sitting room. There is an old oak staircase, and in some of the rooms are massive oak beams, now covered with whitewash. Some 45 years ago, several of the apartments were well fitted up as a shooting box, for the use of the late Earl of Lonsdale.

We had a chat with the farmer, who has held this farm and resided in the hall for many years. He told us that almost the whole of the land was in grass, as pasture or meadow, and that out of 633 acres in all, there were no fewer than 130 acres of meadow to be mown! And this is quite characteristic of the valley of the Eden. The nature of the country between Settle and Kirkby Stephen may be understood from a fact communicated to us by one of the engineers upon the line. As they proceeded in their survey and their work northwards from Settle, they traversed thirty-two miles before they came to a single ploughed field, and that, the first they met with, was a field of potatoes near Bull Ghyll, and close to Kirkby Stephen! Even in the upper Edendale there is little arable land, the greater part being pasture, which is found more suitable to the climate and more profitable to the farmer. There is less land under the plough than there was even a few years ago. Our farmer friend told us that in haytime a labourer on his land earns £2 a week, but that the custom of the country is to hire the farm servants for the period of six months. The labourers, who are mostly on his farm single men, are boarded and lodged in the house, and receive £18 as the half-year's wages.

A footpath across the meadows, and near the Eden, led us to another relic of former times.

Lammerside Castle appears to have no annals; it was formerly known as the Dolorous Tower. The remains stand in the middle of a field between Wharton Hall and Pendragon Castle. They consist of a small square keep and some traces of foundations and walls in the adjoining field. Small apartments, which may have been guard rooms, with vaulted roofs, are now used apparently as shelter for cows. The stone is the common stone of the country. Out of crevices in the walls spring a few wild shrubs and flowers, and scraps of lichen stain the walls with a brighter colour. A few remains of arches, and of window lights may be observed. Still the ruins are lacking in picturesqueness, owing to their solitary situation in the meadow, and the evident removal of all adjuncts which might have interfered with the cultivation of the land. One only thing seems certain, that these and similar ruins are vivid memorials of a bygone state of society, when all this district was again and again the scene of savage border warfare.

Coutinuing our ascent of the valley of the Eden, less than half-an-hour's walking brought us to a spot of historical, and even romantic, interest, and to ruins of some beauty though of no great extent. On a green knoll higher up the valley, and near the little hamlet of Outhgill, rise the picturesque ruins of

Pendragon Castle. At this point the valley runs between the sombre ridge on the east, known as Mallerstang Edge, with a steep escarpment near its summit, and the massive pile of mountain appropriately termed Wild Boar Fell on the west. The Eden pursues its pleasant course among the greenest of meadows and pastures, here overshadowed by trees, and there murmuring over scattered rocks amidst the open dale. As we approached the Castle, we observed the moat, which either was never completed, or more probably, became filled up in places through neglect and decay, and we were reminded of the old couplet, which runs:—

"Let Uther Pendragon do what he can,
Eden will run where Eden ran."

For the tradition is, that Uther endeavoured to perfect the defences of his fortress by leading the waters of the Eden around it, but that all his efforts were ineffectual. This Uther, chroniclers tell us, was surnamed Pendragon, on account of having been likened to a dragon's head by Merlin, the great prophet. He was an eminent warrior, and was father of the famous King Arthur.

The reader will not need to be told that the present ruins date from a period many centuries subsequent to the traditionary events alluded to. There are occasional allusions to Pendragon in authentic history, from the fourteenth century downwards. Many and various were its fortunes. It was burnt by the Scots in 1340, and having been again re-built, was again laid in ruins in 1541; it was rebuilt by the Countess of Pembroke in 1660, and was again all but demolished in 1685 by the Earl of Thanet. This Castle has been held by various families, by Morvilles, Vetriponts, Cliffords, Earls of Pembroke, and Earls of Thanet. "Here Sir Hugh Morville, of a Norman house, lord of Westmoreland, one of the knights implicated in the murder of à Beckett, held his brief but lordly tenure, and his sword was long preserved in Kirkoswald Castle as a memento of the assasination." The Countess of Pembroke, mentioned above as one of the restorers of this edifice, was the masculine woman whose indignant and defiant reply to a minister of the crown, who attempted to force an objectionable candidate upon one of her boroughs, has so often been quoted:—"I have been bullied by an usurper; I have been neglected by a court; but I will not be dictated to by a subject. Your man shall not stand."

The site of so famous a stronghold is now occupied only by the remains of a square keep—a tangle within of mountain ash and wild rose briars, of nettles and long grass, mingling among the disjointed scattered masonry. Hare-bells, blue and white, woodruff, and tansy, grow luxuriantly among the ruins, and the ruefern flourishes amid the crevices of the crumbling walls. Here and there may be observed sandstone coigns of a re-entrant shape, in one block of stone—a peculiarity of old masonry, not likely to be revived in days when castles, if built, are built by contract.

Pendragon Castle can be seen from the railway just on the south of Birkett tunnel; it stands on a knoll rising out of the valley below. From the line just north of the same tunnel, a glimpse is obtained of Lammerside Castle.

After so long a morning, spent in inspecting triumphs of engineering skill and monuments of antiquity, we were not unwilling to direct our steps to the hospitable town of Kirkby Stephen. The highroad was the nearest, and therefore the most welcome. As we skirted the lovely Eden, we could sympathise with Old Drayton's lines:—

> "O, my bright, lovely brook, whose name doth bear the sound
> Of God's first garden plot, th' imparadised ground,
> Wherein he placed man, from whence by sin he fell :
> O, little, blessed brook, how doth my bosom swell
> With love I bear to thee ; the day cannot suffice
> For Mallerstang to gaze upon thy beauteous eyes."

Passing through the ancient village of Nateby, where, as in other dale villages, our hearts were cheered by beholding the rising walls of a spacious board school, we soon reached Stenkreth. At Stenkreth or Stankthred is a noble bridge, which spans the Eden in a most romantic point of its course. Looking below, the visitor sees the river eddying and whirling at a depth of some 70 feet below; the circular holes or "pots" are singular, and deserve observation; they are from one foot to six feet in diameter. The largest is called Coopkarnel hole. Near this spot, it is said, was formerly a narrow fissure, through which the river ran; so narrow that it could be spanned. The story goes that a drunken mason declared that he would be the last to span it, and that he smote the projecting rock with all his might, and broke it, and so fulfilled his foolish word.

A few minutes brought us to the King's Arms, where we found ourselves ready for a substantial luncheon, and in the pleasant garden of which we lounged, enjoying the distant views of the Westmoreland Fells, remarking, to our surprise, the railway train steaming up the distant hill side on its way to Darlington.

Kirkby Stephen, the second town of Westmoreland, is situated in the rich green valley of the Eden, about a mile and a half from the railway station, and about 300 feet below the level of the line. It is a neat town, with a broad, clean street. The houses, some of which are very good, are built of the breccia of the district. There are halls for different societies, and sundry places of worship.

The name Kirkby is indicative of Danish origin, and signifies "church town." Stephen is the name of the patron saint. The spacious and handsome church, the lofty tower of which is conspicuous from every quarter, has recently been very effectively restored. It contains several monuments of interest. We noted especially one, consisting of three full-length alabaster figures, viz., Thomas, the first Lord Wharton, in the middle, and on the right side Eleanor, his first wife, and on the left, his second wife, Anne. On the edge of the monument is a Latin epitaph, which has thus been translated into English rhyme:—

"I, Thomas Wharton, here do lie,
    With my two wives beside me;
    Ellen the first, and Anne the next,
    In Hymen's bonds who tied me.
O, earth! resume my flesh and bones,
    Which back to thee are given;
And then, O God, receive our souls
    To live with Thee in heaven."

A stiff walk of half an hour brought us to the railway station.

Between Settle and Carlisle the only towns of importance are Kirkby Stephen and Appleby. Now, Appleby is a county town, and a famous town, with a castle, and a corporation, and a history! Appleby is not like a town that has just risen —a *nouveau riche*, like Shoddy town in the West Riding, or Cast-iron ville in Cleveland. No! Appleby was famous when these were undreamt of. Though we won't insist upon Julius Cæsar having built the tower which bears his name, is it not a fact, that Henry I. gave Appleby a charter of privileges equal to York, viz., "Freedom from toll, stallage, lastage, and pontage, throughout England, except in the City of London?" The charter of York was granted in the morning, and that of Appleby in the afternoon. A town that was enfranchised by Norman Kings, that wrangled with the Cliffords, treated with the Plantagenets, was burned by the marauding Scots, that defied the Lord Protector Cromwell, that kindled bonfires and drank the King's health at the Restoration, that boasts for its motto "NEC FERRO, NEC IGNI," and has on the reverse of the common seal the figure of St. Lawrence on the gridiron, that was the scene of the famous electoral contects between Brougham and the Lowthers,—such a town, to say nothing of its market, its fairs, and its assizes, is a town that is not to be sneezed at, and we visited it in a due, not to say a subdued, spirit of reverential enquiry.

Appleby, in its general appearance, certainly retains much of its primitive character. It is approached from the railway station by descending a steep hill and crossing the river Eden by a handsome bridge, the views from which, both up and down stream, are very pleasing. A short, narrow street leads from the bridge to the main street of the town, the Borough gate—at right angles to the bridge street. This wide thoroughfare has the cloisters and the church at the bottom, and the castle at the top. There is a pillar (hardly to be termed a town cross), with a fountain, at the lower end of the town; and a similar pillar, with a vane, at the upper end, upon which latter is the inscription—

"RETAIN YOUR LOYALTY;
PRESERVE YOUR RIGHTS."

Very sound, judicious, and safe advice, certainly; but, "the bearing of the remark lies in its application," and what that may be we could not tell. Perhaps one line was contributed by each of the two political parties! The plain old motehouse, standing like a middle row, certainly does not improve the appearance of the street; the public shambles, a little higher up, are a great disfigurement. On the left hand the visitor will observe a row of almshouses; and on the right some old whitewashed and thatched tenements, quite of the olden times. The Tufton Arms is the newest, and most spacious and handsome edifice in Appleby. Here we put up, and found ourselves in very comfortable quarters.

In the morning, having ordered breakfast, we thought we might improve the time by paying a visit to the church; but we must confess that it was not to matins that we went, the modern Anglican customs having apparently not as yet penetrated to Appleby. The church stands in a convenient position at the bottom of the Borough gate, and is approached through cloisters and the church yard. According to the sextoness, the original edifice was erected in 1113, but, it was almost re-built in 1653—of course, by the inevitable Lady Anne Clifford. In fact, during our pilgrimage to Craven and the Settle and Carlisle district, we seem to have never been out of the presence of Lady Anne. Here, in Appleby, Lady Anne has been building almshouses, restoring the church, repairing the castle, and, here in Appleby, Lady Anne is BURIED at last!

A handsome and dignified church it is. The pointed arches are fine, and the highly decorated flat ceiling of 1655 has doubtless its admirers. But what shall we say of the pews sacred to the accommodation of "the quality?" There is the castle pew in its splendour—well, we were so courteously admitted to see the Castle, that we are willing to think the inmates of this pew deserve their comfort. But there is the Corporation pew! Well, the Mayor and Corporation are so ancient that nobody knows when they began to be—so nothing can possibly be too good for them. No! our municipal institutions deserve to be treated with something more than respect. So, after all, though we were a little disposed to rebel, in a radical spirit, against the dignities of Appleby Church, it appears that "whatever is, is right!"

Bnt the glory of Appleby Church is not its handsome pews, or its handsome ceiling, or its old bibles, with the links still left with which they were wont to be chained to the desk. No! something more glorious than all these is here. Here is a marble monument and effigy to Lady Margaret—a Russell by birth, and a daughter of an Earl of Bedford—and a Clifford by marriage, to wit, the Countess of an Earl of Cumberland—and, above, all this, mother of Lady Anne! But even this monument, imposing as it is, is not the flower and crown, the *ne plus ultra* of Appleby Church.

HERE IS THE TOMB OF LADY ANNE!

A black marble monument records her grandeur, in whose veins flowed the blood of the Cliffords and the Russells, who married successively the Earl of Dorset and the Earl of Pembroke. Here, in splendid array, are spread before the eyes of posterity the arms of all the Cliffords. So the old countess was but mortal! In Skipton Castle she first saw the light, and no she-wolf ever fought more fiercely for her young than Lady Anne for her barony of Skipton. Many a castle did she rebuild: Skipton, Pendragon, and Appleby remain to prove her "the restorer of waste places to dwell in." "Crosses and contradictions" had she with two husbands; and, however uncharitable the supposition may be, we cannot but think her husbands must have had "crosses and contradictions" with her! She had been "neglected by a court, and bullied by an usurper," but the old lioness was "not to be dictated to by a subject!" we trow not, indeed! However, though she braved it out, saw the work of her hands, and "lay," now in this castle, and now in that, of her own building and her own property, she succumbed at last at the ripe age of 87. And the historian tells of her, that "her house was a school for the young, a retreat for the aged, an asylum for the persecuted, a college for the learned, and a pattern for all." Nor must we forget that she erected the monument we have all seen in Westminster Abbey to the memory of our great poet, Edmund Spenser; and we have the testimony of Bishop Rainbow to her worth, and not to her character only, but to her tongue, for he says, in his funeral sermon for her ladyship quoting Dr. Donne, (and we can well believe it), that "sh could talk well on all subjects, from predestination to slea silk." And here she lies, in her own country, and among the scenes she knew, and the sacred shrines and princely homes she edified or re-edified while she was yet "in the flesh."

Appleby Castle is at present the residence of Admiral Elliott, who acts as steward to Sir Henry Tufton, whose estates in Yorkshire and Westmoreland are extensive. Wishing to see the old keep. we ventured, although it was only nine in the morning, as our time was short, to apply for admission. At the top of the street is the entrance to the castle grounds; indeed. the street leads nowhere else, and there is nothing to do but to follow the example of the Duke of York:—

"The Duke of York and all his men
Went up the hill and down again."

Applying at the modern stone house where the Admiral lives, we were readily permitted to see the old tower known as Cæsar's tower,—for what reason no one on earth seems to know. It is near the house, just across the lawn, in a north-westerly direction. It is a square, battlemented keep, with four turrets at the angles, each turret surmounted by a vane. The walls are partially mantled with ivy, in the very trimmest possible condition. The apartments are utterly neglected, some being empty, and some used for storing timber.

Climbing to the top of one of the turrets, we enjoyed a splendid prospect. The castle is perfectly embowered in plantations of ashes, walnuts, horse-chestnuts, and (what are not common in this district) elm trees. The foliage altogether hides the little town below, but beyond the walls, and the moat, and the plantations, the country stretches in every direction, and each prospect has some feature of interest or of charm. Looking to the west and north-west, we recognized the mountains of the lake district; eastward rises the massive range of Cross Fell; to the south the horizon is bounded by the mountains of north-west Yorkshire, whilst on the north the view is more limited by the rising ground in the vicinity. The Midland Railway may be traced in its progress from Settle to Carlisle, and is in view for many miles of its course.

Having seen the church and the castle, we conceived that we had "done" Appleby, and we left it, feeling that its interest lies more in the past chronicles it boasts than in any existing splendour such as is wont to adorn the county towns of our country. But what can be expected from a town which has never gone a-head, but has been incontinently burned down by those restless and marauding Scots? Such a fate was enough, surely, to discourage, in some slight measure, even so gallant and stout-hearted citizens as the good burgesses of Appleby.

A very interesting and enjoyable excursion in the county of Cumberland, may be made from Lazonby,--including Kirkoswald and the far-famed Nunnery Walks. Descending from Lazonby Station into the valley, we crossed the fine bridge over the Eden, here of 60 or 70 yards in width, and followed the lane towards Kirkoswald. Before reaching the town, we turned to the left by a paved path leading through a noble avenue of lime trees towards the parish church. This lies at the foot of a hill, on the top of which is the campanile tower, with three bells. It struck us as odd, though there are similar cases elsewhere, that the tower and the church should be placed at so great a distance one from the other. The church consists of a nave, with aisles, which are of the Transition period, from Norman to Early English. There are monuments and brasses to various members of the family of Featherstonehaugh, who have been settled here since the time of James I.

At the west end of the church, below the west window, is a well, supplied from a spring which issues from the hill, and flows under the church. A chain and iron vessel are provided that the traveller may slake his thirst from this most ecclesiastical source. The steps down to the well are within a decayed enclosure of wooden paling.

In the churchyard are many gravestones, with curious inscribed memorial brasses let into them, after the custom of the country. These seem all to be of the present and the last centuries. There are also two ancient gravestones of some interest, both with crosses, one with a cross fleurée and shears.

Before entering the town, we visited the ruins of the ancient Castle of Kirkoswald, which will be found adjoining a lane leading from the high road, a little east of the town. The broken, uneven ground tells of the former extent and importance of the fortress. Among ashes and sycamores are many fragments and some large portions of masonry still remaining. The largest mass yet standing is what remains of an ancient tower; it may be sixty feet in height, and has small embrasured windows looking without, and large windows apparently of apartments which faced the castle yard. We saw a melancholy horse emerge from what was once a dungeon, but is now a stable or cow-house, fitted up with mangers and troughs. We failed to recognise in the animal any signs of breeding which might indicate descent from any of the caparisoned and high-mettled war steeds which must once have gone forth, prancing in their pride, from those castle gates, on errands of warfare, or in quest of booty, or to repel a foray from the north.

This castle was originally founded about 1201 by Randolph Eugayne; was greatly improved by Sir Hugh Morville and succeeding owners, and especially by the Dacres.

Kirkoswald is the best point from which to visit the celebrated and beautiful grounds of The Nunnery. After partaking of an abundant luncheon at the little homely inn, the Featherstone Arms, we availed ourselves of the kind services of Mr. Milton, who makes his home at the inn, and who, having lived as butler with the neighbouring family for many years, is well acquainted with the country, and is disposed to assist the tourist with his knowledge and guidance.

It is a pleasant walk across the fields, and by the manor house of Staffold, to the nunnery. The original convent was founded by William Rufus. At the dissolution of monasteries the property belonging to the convent was granted to the family of Graham, from whom it passed into the hands of the Aglionbys, who have held it for nearly two centuries. The house, which is of red sandstone, was built in 1715. It commands a fine view eastward.

The key of the Walks, which are readily made accessible to visitors, may be obtained at the house. We passed under a row of spruce firs, the finest trees of the kind we remember to have seen, as well as a stately row of beech trees. The Walks border not only the river Eden, but a beck, the Croglin, which, at this point pours its tributary flood into the river. This part of the romantic scenery of the Nunnery has been thus accurately and vigorously described:—"It may, we think, be safely asserted that the Croglin, in this last part of its course, for the space of a mile, during which it pours along a deep ravine, has no equal. It first enters this savage dell by a fall of 40 feet, forcing its way through a cleft into a deep caldron, scooped out of the rock, in which the water is agitated and whirled round in boiling eddies, till it finds an escape by a narrow opening in one corner, whence it rushes down several leaps, foaming over the large masses that hinder its impetuous progress. The rocks are piled upon each other to the height of 100 or 200 feet, projecting their bold fronts forward over the river, 'here scorched with lightning, there with ivy green,' or grey with aged lichens and mosses. On the other side the path is carried round the protruding masses of rock on rudely framed galleries supported by rough timbers, thus affording the best and most striking views, because the rocks and woods on Mr. Aglionby's ground, which are the grandest, are seen to the best advantage. At one time you are on the margin of the water, beneath overhanging crags, the brook before you rushing furiously over moss-coloured fragments and stones, forming cascades of exceeding beauty, whilst the trees, waving in the breeze, reveal the shaggy rock that supplies their roots with scanty nourishment. At another, you are on the brink of the precipice, looking down into a dense mass of wood, out of which the twisted branches of the rift oak, stripped of their bark, 'toss their giant arms amid the skies,' contrasting with the deep green behind, while the water is betrayed by its sparkling sheen and softened roar." This language, though strong, is not exaggerated. The beauty of the Nunnery

Walks is not exceeded, either by the Torrent Walk at Dolgelly, or the Meeting of the Waters at Lynmouth.

The following are the chief points of interest:—The waterfall plunging down into the wooded glen; the bower overlooking the river—a favourite spot for luncheon; a greensward lower down, where gipsy parties boil the kettle and prepare tea, and where *al fresco* dances are frequently got up by youthful visitors; the walk over the rocks and beneath the cliffs overhanging the river. The Eden is here some sixty yards in width, and is a good salmon stream, especially for young fish; opposite is Samson's Chamber, a large cave overlooking the river, into which you crawl on hands and knees. Samson's chuckie-chuckie stone is not far distant. Just above the chamber is the Settle and Carlisle line, the construction of which, at this spot was a work of great difficulty, owing to the crumbling and unstable character of the soil.

Upon our return to Kirkoswald we admired the fertile meadows and pastures through which we passed, and were told by our guide that the usual rent of land is about 40s. or 45s. an acre; but that some exceptionally good meadow land in this valley lets at £8 an acre! We passed through the fields of one farmer who grazes 3000 sheep. The aspect of the country speaks of plenty and prosperity.

A good walker may extend this excursion to Armathwaite, where is the modernized castle, which was for centuries the home of the Skeltons, and the situation of which is very romantic, among the rocky wooded heights overlooking the course of the Eden.

If, however, the visitor return to Lazonby station, he should endeavour to make a pilgrimage to "Long Meg and her Daughters,"—interesting remains of British Druidism, situated about half a mile south of the church of Addingham, on a very elevated site.

The remains consist of 67 unhewn upright stones, forming a circle 350 feet in diameter. The stones are of different formations, and "there is great disparity in their height and sizes, for while some of them are ten feet high above the ground, and fifteen or sixteen feet in circumference, others are not more than two or three feet in height. Many of them are now prostrate on the ground." Meg herself stands eighteen feet high, and is fifteen feet in girth round her waist, and her four angles face the four points of the compass.

CHAPTER XIII.

GEOLOGY OF CRAVEN.*

THE district to which the preceding pages profess to be a Guide includes the greater part of the Deanery of Craven, and a portion of the Archdeaconry of Richmond, or, in other words, of nearly the whole of the Wapontake of Staincliffe, and a part of Ewcross; Horton in Ribblesdale, Clapham, Ingleton, and Thornton being in the latter Wapontake. Bingley, and parts of Addingham and Keighley are in Skirack, and a part of Ilkley in Claro; the four latter are included in Craven by Dr. Whitaker, but are only incidentally mentioned in this volume. It may here be noticed that the derivations of Craven—British *Craigvan*, the district of rocks, and Staincliffe—Anglo Saxon *Ston* and *Clyff*, are nearly identical.

This district has always held a high rank with regard to the attractive character of its scenery, and those peculiar natural features which invariably accompany the massive deposits and dislocations of mountain limestone; and to the Geologist, the Mineralogist, the Antiquarian, and the Botanist, as well as to the lover of Landscape, presents a field of no ordinary interest.

As the nature, character, and extent of the various strata which compose a district are so intimately connected with scenic effects, a sketch, at least, of the Geology becomes a necessary part of the Topographer's task—a task in the present instance rendered comparatively easy by the accurate researches and admirable work of Professor Phillips on the Geology of Yorkshire. In the recognised order then the Silurian first claims attention.

* This Chapter on the Geology of the district is taken from Howson's Guide to Craven, with slight additions and alterations.

SILURIAN.

The great mass of Silurian which forms Hougill and Casterton Fells is bordered on the east by the range of the Pennine Fault, as far south as Kirkby Lonsdale, where the Pennine turns suddenly to the E.S.E. and receives the name of the Craven Fault. Near Ingleton the Fault splits into two; the northern branch running by the north end of Clapham Tarn, Austwick, Stainforth, and Malham Tarn, whilst the southern takes its course by Clapham Village, Austwick (south end) Buckhaw Brow and Giggleswick Scars, through Giggleswick and Settle, up Stockdale and on eastwards by the foot of Malham Cove through Skirethorn, and crosses the Wharfe near Grassington. The Silurian rocks appear north of the northern Fault, where the rivers have cut down to them, the greatest spread being in the valley of the Ribble, from Stainforth to above Horton and westwards to the valley lying between Moughton and Norber,— and south of it on the south east of Malham Tarn. For miles in length the junction of the nearly level surface of the Silurian and the great plateau of Lower Scar Limestone which supports Whernside, Ingleborough and Penyghent may be distinctly seen, and the fissures, joints, and laminæ of the supporting slate, with the horizontal beds and vertical joints of the limestone are very striking. In its course from Kirkby Lonsdale the Silurian forms a remarkable hollow between the limestone hills, reaches a height of 750 feet, three miles above Ingleton, and attains an elevation of 1166 feet, under the south front of Moughton. In Casterton Fells it rises to a height of 1400 feet, and in Hougill Fells 2220 feet. In the latter Fells the peculiar scenic effects of the Silurian are well displayed; there it forms high conical hills, with steep, smooth, and regular slopes, meeting in narrow and angular valleys, and covered with a green coarse herbage. Although narrow and depressed between the Craven Faults, its appearance beneath the horizontal limestone at Moughton, Norber, Ingleton, and more especially at Thornton Foss produces singular effects in the landscape.

The great change of mineral character and structure between the slates of Ingleton and Ribblesdale, along the same line of stratification, is very remarkable; and not less interesting is the spectacle of their complete overthrow to nearly vertical positions. and the subsequent wearing down of their surface to a singularly even plane.

In the blue roofing slates of Ingleton the cleavage planes present a constant course to the S.E., dipping slightly to the S.W., whilst cross joints run vertically to the N., and oblique joints dip to the N.E. Some of the cleavage planes are covered with arborescent films, and cubical crystals of iron pyrites are commonly met with.

Besides the dykes in connection with the Whin in Tynedale and Teesdale, two interposed igneous rocks only have been observed in Yorkshire, and these are at Ingleton; the most distinct being only a few feet wide, and projecting like a wall from the left bank of the Greta about one hundred yards below the slate quarries. The composition of the stone is peculiar; red felspar, occasionally in large masses, hornblende and mica, sometimes in broad flakes; it is commonly called greenstone, but more properly micaceous syenite.

The Ribblesdale Slates, which correspond with the "Coniston Flags" of Professor Sedgwick, are widely expanded, and have been worked at many points, and perhaps a finer flag-stone is nowhere found. In the quarries under Moughton, on Swarth Moor, and at Studfold, the position and structure of the rock may be readily observed. Of the two sets of planes which divide the rock into rhomboidal prisms, the one called *spires* is very obvious, and separates the rock into tables of great extent and uniform thickness; the other, more indistinct, is called *bate*, and may be considered to be the laminar structure, whilst the spires are the planes of stratification. It is quarried in a peculiar manner, with attention not only to the structure, but to the situation and dryness, and the joints, nodules, limited depth of the tabular separations, &c., make the quarrying rather a hazardous speculation. The thickness of these flags in Ribblesdale is supposed to be not less than two thousand feet.

Mountain Limestone.

Phillips divides this series into two general types by a line drawn through Kettlewell to Ryeloaf, and thence westwards to Lancaster, and he states his belief that this line divides the oceanic from the littoral portion of the great limestone deposit. The following table is necessary in order to understand the two series and their subdivisions.

NORTHERN SERIES.	SOUTHERN SERIES.
UPPER GROUP, (Yoredale Rocks of Phillips) composed of { Limestone. Coal. Laminated Grit. Limestone. Shale.	UPPER GROUP. { Black laminated Limestone & Shale LOWER GROUP. | Nearly undivided.
LOWER GROUP, (Scar Limestone). { Partially divided by shales.	

NORTHERN SERIES.—*Lower Group.* Commencing with the widest expanse and greatest thickness (1000 feet) of the Lower Scar Limestone, it is found to fill Kettlewelldale from Buckden, it then turns up Littondale almost to its source, and covering Hardflask, forms a general base of Fountains Fell, Scoska Moor, and Penyghent, thus uniting Wharfedale with Ribblesdale. The southern boundary of this great area passes along a line of dislocation from Threshfield to Malham, and, bending to the north round Ryeloaf, is continued to Settle. Its lofty escarpments then turn along the course of the Ribble as far as Stainforth, where the slate is brought up to the surface by the northern branch of the Craven Fault. Beyond, it again resumes its parallelism to the river, and three miles above Horton fills the whole valley. Again to the south and west it presents a great undulated floor of bare limestone rocks around the slopes of Ingleborough, and borders the valleys at Wharfe, Clapham, and Ingleton, with magnificent and continuous scars. This vast range, together with the southern one which is traced by Giggleswick Scar, Feizor, Austwick, Newby, and Ingleton, marks the double line of dislocation, so well known by the name of the Great Craven Fault.

Throughout this large area the limestone rock is nearly undivided, and presents one vast calcareous mass four or five hundred feet thick, and this mighty range is but the edge of a plateau, which underlies the whole of the elevated region from Wharfedale to the valley of the Tyne. With regard to the extent of the dislocations caused by the Craven Faults, it was thought by Professor Phillips, that the northern drop is about three hundred feet, whilst the total depression under Ingleborough is not less than three thousand feet, about Settle one thousand, and it diminishes towards Grassington, where numerous other dislocations confuse but do not destroy its effects. The limestone beds are not usually conspicuous along the line of the axis of disturbance; enough however can be seen to assure us that while the elevated beds rise slightly to the Fault, the depressed beds fall steeply to the south; they are no where vertical, and the angle of their inclination continually diminishes eastwards. From the point where the southern Fault becomes distinct in Giggleswick Scar there is a very violent southward dip of the depressed beds; and at Feizor, Kirkby Fell, and Malham Moors the elevated beds rise slightly to this Fault. At Giggleswick the lower level limestone is opposed to the inclined millstone grit of Ingleborough, indicating a slip of one thousand feet; and the same is the case at Ryeloaf and Brown Hill.

Malham Tarn is on the line of the great northern slip, three hundred feet below the bold escarpment; the Cove is parallel to the southern Fault. The valley from Malham downwards is full of dislocations and varying dips, especially at Kirkby Malham, the general result being a dip of the depressed beds from the great Fault for one mile, and then a rise in the same direction, so as to expose a considerable tract of the Upper Craven Limestone about Calton, Otterburn, Coniston, and Eshton, thus connecting them with the range of Limestone, by Flasby, Rylstone, and Burnsall. The hollow caused by the southern slip reaches Wharfedale between Kilnsey and Threshfield, where it falls into another system of dislocations, having had an uninterrupted course from Northumberland to Wharfedale, a distance of one hundred and thirty miles.

It is the Lower Scar Limestone chiefly which gives to the district of Craven those marked features which must always interest the lover of landscape and the geologist. It produces the characteristic scenery of Bolland, Wharfedale, Upper Airedale, and Ribblesdale. And the Scars along its southern edge rearing their barrier-fronts along the pastoral dales, form a magnificent base and foreground for the lofty mountains which rise above them.

In general, broad surfaces, mighty cliffs, frequent and deep clefts, chasms, and caves, constitute the typical character of this lower limestone floor. To it Gordale owes all its magnificence, whilst other cascades, as Thornton and Scaleber, owe much of their distinctive features to the top of the fall only being guarded by a durable ledge of limestone, and the lower parts filled with wasting argillaceous beds. The caves are most frequent where the limestone is thickest, and not divided by shales or grits, and so elevated as to permit the water to pass down, or to justify the suspicion that in some former condition it may have passed. They mainly owe their extent, enlargement, or modification to the eroding influence of springs and subterraneous streams. The joints and bedding planes which so numerously intersect the rock no doubt facilitate this excavating process, and those which have a flat roof, indicating a bedding plane, are generally found to be the most roomy and of the greatest extent.

Upper Group, or Yoredale Rocks. In the upper part of Wensleydale this series has the greatest degree of complexity and attains the thickness of one thousand feet, and nearly the same particulars of complexity are found in Whernside. In Ingleborough this series is composed of about one thonsand feet of limestones, plates and laminated grits; and near the top is a crinoidal limestone forming a prominent scar, thirty feet thick, called the Main Limestone, covered with alternating grits and plates; and the whole is crowned with a pebbly millstone grit. In Penyghent, also, and Fountains Fell, the main limestone occurs under a cover of the same grit, surmounted by shales and flagstones, with coal.

Between the Craven Fault and Upper Wharfedale the Yoredale series partially covers a large oval space of lower limestone, and is much elevated, including Birks, Litton Hill, Raisgill Hag, Cam, Cosh Knot, Hardflask, Scoska, &c.

The variations in the series which compose the Yoredale rocks produce corresponding effects in the landscape. In general, the limestones always project, argillaceous beds form straight, undulated or obscure slopes, and the grit occasionally makes rough angular edges; this latter, indeed, is so mixed with plate that it does not often assume the character which it does under more favourable circumstances. In Ingleborough and Penyghent the main limestone projects into a mural precipice, and below it there is a uniform slope of several hundred feet. In Bowland, and south of the Craven Fault, the series being almost wholly shale, with interlaminated limestones in its lower part, presents only sloping surfaces below the grit summits, and smooth rounded hills in all the large region between Ribblesdale and the border of the Yorkshire coalfield. Although the lower limestone produces those grand escarpments which guard the dales, the facility of waste in the Yoredale series has cleared their broad surfaces, formed many extensive denudations and insular hills, and is the cause of much of the grandeur and peculiarity of the district.

SOUTHERN SERIES.—*Lower Limestone*. The lower limestone occupies a considerable extent of country in the vale of the Hodder, and in Bowland. It fills oval spaces in the midst of a mountain country whose higher parts are surmounted with millstone grit, and the intermediate slopes are formed with shales and grits. It is not from the lowness of this part of Craven that the limestone comes to day; it is in fact uplifted, for the country S.W. of the Craven Fault has its own system of disturbances, consisting of anticlinal axes, and whilst the northern dislocations are remarkable for sudden and violent fracture and partial displacement, the southern consist only of steep anticlinal ridges, causing a long system of parallel undulations and contortions, and giving to the district its most striking features.

The principal mass of this limestone shows itself in the Trough of Bowland, Slaidburn, Whitewell, Downham, Rimington, and Lothersdale.

Upper Group. The dark laminated limestone of Craven appears as much connected with the shale above as with the lower member of the mountain limestone. It may be considered as forming a passage into the Yoredale series.

An excellent section of these beds is seen in the quarry of the Leeds and Liverpool Canal near Thornton, where alternations of calcareous and argillaceous beds rest upon a thick mass of laminated and crinoidal limestone. Similar beds occur at Gisburne, Broughton, in the quarries near Skipton and in Lothersdale, and in the valley between Skipton and Bolton Abbey. North of Skipton is another line of nearly parallel elevated limestone, ranging from Flasby, by Craco and Burnsal, towards Nidderdale, and dipping distinctly beneath the grit summits of Rylstone and Flasby Fells. Northwards it expands largely up Kettlewelldale and Langstrothdale, whilst in Littondale and at Kilnsey it joins the great limestone plateau of Malham Moors. The thickness of the limestone exposed between Kettlewell and Great Whernside is about nine hundred feet. It is often liable to a local change into a crystallized yellowish rock, full of nodules and cells of calcareous spar; in this state it is called by the miners "dun lime," and is said to destroy the productiveness of the mineral veins.

The shales, which represent the Yoredale series, occupy a large area in the southern part of Craven; extending east and west from Bolton Abbey to Bowland, and north and south from

Ryeloaf to Pendle. The best exhibitions of this series may be seen in the Trough of Bowland, on the west front of Pendle in the Hodder near Stonyhurst, in its upper sources above Slaidburn, and in various parts of the Ribble between Clitheroe and Settle. It covers the limestone ridges of Lothersdale, Skipton and Craco, is rich in fossils at Flasby, curiously contorted at Bolton Abbey, and is almost universally found beneath the pastures in the lower and central parts of Craven. Its thickness below Pendle Hill and at Skipton is about four thousand feet, but in Bowland probably less. A good description of these beds is given in the Geological Survey Memoir, " On the Burnley Coalfield, &c."

Millstone Grit.

The millstone grit rests on the Yoredale series; both consist of limestones, sandstones, shales, ironstones, and thin coal seams, but while limestones abound in the lower series, sandstones predominate in the upper, and the limestones become almost obliterated. Their common boundary is thus not easy to be determined. In all the Bowland district above the limestone masses lies one very thick gritstone group, and from the Lancaster side of Bowland it passes by an easy gradation to the more varied series of grit on the west of the Lune, a series intermediate between those of Ingleborough and Bowland. South of the Craven Faults is a narrow band of elevated gritstone country, which from Giggleswick and Settle eastwards presents a singular rivalry to the limestone band between the Faults. Thus, at Giggleswick the grit is opposed to the limestone, both one thousand feet ; so Ryeloaf, one thousand seven hundred and ninety five feet, opposes the limestones of Kirkby Fell, one thousand eight hundred feet ; and the grit of Brown Hill, one thousand two hundred and fifty eight feet, meets the limestone of Boardley, one thousand three hundred and fifty two feet. It crowns most of the hills between Whernside in Ingleton Fells and Great and Little Whernside in Kettlewelldale, and ranging by Grassington, exists in great force in Flasby, Rylstone. and Burnsal Fells, appears at the Strid and Bolton Bridge, and on the southern bank of the Wharfe, from near Harewood to Skipton, forms the outcrop of the floor of the Great Yorkshire Coal Field.

The millstone grit is an important element in the scenery of the eastern and western boundary and high summits of Craven. Its elevation and structure, and the coldness and humidity of the climate favour the growth of heath and sedgy grass, which almost extirpate other vegetation, and form a surface of dreary moorlands, far less serviceable to the agriculturalist than much loftier hills of slate. It is often concealed, except in torrents, but sometimes the escarpments appear in bold craggy fronts, which from their wasting and ruinous appearance, may well rival in interest the famous Granite Tors of Devonshire. Bowland Knotts will well repay a visit.

Coal.

The singular coal field in the low valley of the Greta, between Ingleton and Burton, bears a complete analogy to the field on the South Tyne. Both are far detached from the large tracts to which they appear related; both range east and west, and both lie at the foot of an escarpment of rocks much older than themselves, and rest on the same rocks sunk by dislocation, in one case, more than two thousand feet.

The Ingleton bed is not a basin as would at first sight appear, deposited after a dislocation, for the planes of stratification have only a north-eastern dip, which is not the original position, but owing to the Faults making depressions to the south. It has only one outcrop visible to the south, the western is obscured by drifts, and the north-east edge is sunk deep, and terminates on the plane of the south Craven Fault. On the west and south the subjacent grit comes to the surface, and it is seen on the south and south-west that at this insulated spot, two thousand feet below the summit of Ingleborough, some of the lower strata of the far distant Lancashire and Yorkshire Coalfields lie not only above the millstone grit of Penyghent and Ingleborough, but even above rocks usually several hundred feet above them in the scale of strata. At the Burton end the beds are not cut off by any Fault, but are said to thin off to nothing.

The dip of the coal is northerly; two workable seams occur, the upper and best four feet thick, another, forty yards deeper has a thickness of from seven to ten feet. It is remarkable that in the deep coal there are two parallel layers of light blue pipe-clay, with a pure jet or cannel coal between them. The extent of the coalfield to the north of the Greta has never yet been fairly tried. Rising from below the Ingleton coalfield in the direction of Bolland, is a series of millstone grits and shales, enclosing two coal seams, which have been worked, besides others of less thickness. They have been worked at Bentham, Mewith, Tatham, Smear Hall, Clintsfield, &c.

MINERAL PRODUCTIONS.

It is evident from the local abundance of mineral veins in the neighbourhood of great lines of Fault and their paucity in the undisturbed limestones, that they have a near connection with systems of dislocation. Accordingly we find that mineral veins are frequent in Craven. Productive veins of lead have been found in Bowland, at Whitewell and Brennand, Grassington, Kettlewell, Arncliffe, Buckden, and Malham. In the mountain limestones occur the sulphides of lead, copper, iron, and zinc; the oxide of iron; and an oxide of zinc, in the form of a white powder is found at Malham. At Grassington and Kettlewell there are productive ores of lead both in the limestone and millstone grit. A green phosphate of lead is occasionally found on Grassington Moor. The carbonate of zinc, or calamine, has been raised in the compact and pseudomorphous forms at Arncliffe, Kettlewell, and Malham, in large quantities. The sulphuret of iron or iron pyrites occurs plentifully in the slate quarries at Ingleton, and in some of the mines. Hydrous peroxide of iron, or brown hæmatite is found among the broken stones and in the soil under Giggleswick Scar; and bog iron ore, a variety of hæmatite, but of recent formation, has been found on Blea Moor. Ironstone nodules intersected by septa of carbonate of lime, called septaria, are found on Rathmell Moor, and more especially of great size and beauty in Kettlesbeck, near Eldroth, where they have been washed out of the shale beds by the flood. Quartz in clear and regular but small crystals, is found plentifully in the hills above Settle, and darkly coloured with iron, on Giggleswick Scars. Calcareous spar is abundant in the mineral veins, and the stalactite forms will be found in beautiful variety in most of the numerous caverns, but more especially in the Ingleborough Cave, the most instructive cavern, perhaps, in the kingdom.

CHAPTER XIV.

Botany of Craven.

THE plants named in the following list are less common plants to be found within a radius of from ten to fifteen miles around Settle. A local Flora is to be obtained from the publisher of this work.

RANUNCULACEÆ.
Thalictrum minus. Giggleswick Scar Gordale.
flavum. Frequent
Ranunculus auricomus. Clapdale
Trollius europæus. Malham Cove Stainforth Force
Helleborus viridis. Wharfe
fœtidus. Feizor
Aquilegia vulgaris. Stainforth
Actœa spicata. Ingleborough, Malham, Penyghent

NYMPHÆACEÆ.
Nuphar lutea. Ribble

PAPAVERACEÆ.
Papaver dubium. Occasional
Meconopsis cambrica. Stackhouse
Corydalis claviculata. Settle
Corydalis lutea. Langcliffe

CRUCIFERÆ.
Thlaspi alpestre Lead Mines, on the way to Malham
Hutchinsia petræa. Malham Tarn
Lepidium campestre. Settle
Cochlearia officinalis. Frequent
alpina. do.

Draba incana. Attermire
muralis. Malham, &c.
Cardamine amara. Horton, &c.
impatiens. Giggleswick Scar
Sisymbrium Thalianum
Arabis hirsuta. Kelcowe
Barbarea prœcox. Stackhouse
Hesperis matronalis. Settle, Gargrave

RESEDACEÆ.
Reseda luteola. Giggleswick.
lutea. do.

CISTACEÆ.
Helianthemum canum. Malham Cove

VIOLACEÆ.
Viola odorata. Settle Bridge
palustris. Horton, Huntworth
hirta. Kelcowe
lutea Malham Moor

DROSERACEÆ.
Drosera rotundifolia. Helwith Moss

CARYOPHYLLACEÆ.
Saponaria officinalis. Austwick
Silene maritima. Kilnsey Crag and Whernside
Lychnis vespertina. Occasional

Arenaria verna.	Lead Mines
Stellaria nemorum.	Trow Gill and Rathmell
glauca.	Malham Tarn
uliginosa.	Giggleswick
Cerastium semidecandrum.	
triviale.	

MALVACEÆ.

Malva moschata.	Bolton Abbey
rotundifolia.	Thornton

HYPERICACEÆ.

Hypericum humifusum.	Giggleswick Scar
hirsutum.	do.
montanum.	Gordale

GERANIACEÆ.

Geranium phœum.	Wharfe, Clapham
sylvaticum.	Bolton Abbey and Malham
impatiens	Paper Mill
parviflora	Langcliffe
sanguineum.	Ltl. Stainforth

CELASTRACEÆ.

Euonymus Europæus.	Feizor

RAMNACEÆ.

Rhamnus catharticus.	Giggleswick Scar

LEGUMINOSÆ.

Lotus major.	Settle
Ononis spinosa.	Austwick
Trifolium filiforme	Settle
Hippocrepis comosa.	GiggleswkScar
Vicia sylvatica.	Birkwith, Horton
cracca.	Settle
Lathyrus pratensis.	do.
macrorrhizus.	Giggleswick

ROSACEÆ.

Dryas octopetala.	Arncliffe
Potentilla verna.	Kelcowe
alpestris.	Gordale.
Rubus chamœmorus.	Ryeloaf
saxatilis.	Clapdale, &c.
Rosa spinosissima.	Cave Ha' Wood
villosa.	Stackhouse
inodora.	Cave Ha' Wood
micrantha.	Lodge Gill
Sabini.	Ingleton
arvensis.	Rathmell
Poterium sanguisorba.	Giggleswick Scar
Pyrus aria.	Horton, &c.
torminalis.	do.

ONAGRACEÆ.

Epilobium alpinum	Ingleborough
palustre.	do.

PORTULACEÆ.

Montia fontana.	Common

GROSSULARIACEÆ.

Ribes alpinum.	Stainforth

CRASSULACEÆ.

Sedum Rhodiola.	Penyghent
villosum.	Swarth Moor

SAXIFRAGACEÆ.

Saxifraga umbrosa.	Ling Gill
aizoides.	Chapel-le-dale, Ingleborough
oppositifolia.	Penyghent
Geum	Weathercote
stellaris.	Ingleborough
hypnoides.	Winskill Scar
Chrysosplenium alternifolium	Common
Parnassia palustris.	Catterick Force

UMBELLIFERÆ.

Helosciadium nodiflorum.	
	Giggleswick
Pimpinella saxifraga.	Common
magna.	do.
Sium angustifolium.	Settle
Œnanthe crocata.	Rathmell
Silaus pratensis	
Myrrhis odorata.	Frequent
Sanicula Europæa	Stackhouse

CAPRIFOLIACEÆ.

Sambucus Ebulus.	Austwick

RUBIACEÆ.

Galium saxatile.	Giggleswick Scar
sylvestre.	Malham, &c.
boreale.	Kilnsey & Malham

VALERIANACEÆ.

Valerianella olitoria.	Stainforth Scar

DIPSACEÆ.
Scabiosa columbaria — Settle
Knautia arvensis — do.

COMPOSITÆ.
Tragopogon pratensis — Settle, Horton
Hypochæris radicata — do.
Lactuca muralis — Settle, Stackhouse
Crepis virens — Settle
  succisæfolia — Stainforth
  paludosa — Banks of Ribble
Hieracium vulgatum — do.
  Lawsoni — Stockdale
  prenanthoides — Stainforth Force
  boreale — Ribble Banks
  umbellatum — Settle
Serratula tinctoria — Clapham
Carduus Marianus — Bolton Abbey
  heterophyllus — Stackhouse, Feizor
Carlina vulgaris — Settle Hills, &c.
Antennaria dioica — Giggleswick Scar
Gnaphalium sylvaticum — Merebeck
  uliginosum — Eldroth
Senecio sylvaticus — Cocket Moss
  viscosus — Settle
  erucæfolius — Runley Bridge
  Saracenicus — Ingleton
Matricaria Parthenium — Lawkland
  inodora — Malham
Inula dysenterica — Merebeck
Chrysanthemum segetum — Rathmell

CAMPANULACEÆ.
Campanula hederacea — Gargrave
Jasione montana — Rathmell

ERICAEÆ.
Andromeda polifolia — Horton
Vaccinium Vitis Idœa — Ryeloaf
Pyrola minor — Clapdale, Malham

OLEACEÆ.
Ligustrum vulgare — GiggleswickScars

APOCYNACEÆ.
Vinca minor — Buckhaw Brow

GENTIANACEÆ.
Gentiana amarella — GiggleswickScar
Menyanthes trifoliata — HelwithBridge
Polemonium cæruleum — Gordale

SCROPHULARIACEÆ.
Veronica serpyllifolia — Common
  anagallis — Giggleswick
  agrestis — Frequent
  montana — Crow Nest, &c.
Bartsia Alpina — Malham
Melampyrum sylvaticum — Giggleswick
Mimulus luteus — Horton

OROBANCHACEÆ.
Orobanche rubra — Attermire
  minor — Malham
Lathræa squamaria — Cave Ha' Wood

LABIATÆ.
Mentha viridis — Ribble Banks
  sativa — Settle
  piperita — Giggleswick
  arvensis — do.
Origanum vulgare — Winskill Scar
Lamium amplexicaule — Settle
  incisum — do.
Galeopsis tetrahit — Common
  versicolor — Settle
Calamintha Clinopodium — do.
Stachys Betonica — Frequent
  palustris — Settle
  sylvatica — do.
Scutellaria galericulata — Rathmell

VERBENACEÆ.
Verbena officinalis — Wennington

BORAGINEÆ.
Myosotis repens — Penyghent
Lithospermum officinale — Crow Nest
Symphytum tuberosum — Ribble
Anchusa sempervirens — Wharfe, &c.

PRIMULACEÆ.
Primula farinosa — Common
Anagallis tenella — Rathmell

PLUMBAGINACEÆ.
Armeria maritima — Stockdale

PLANTAGINACEÆ.
Plantago maritima — Kilnsey

CHENOPODIACEÆ.
Chenopodium rubrum — Common
Atriplex patula — Ribble Bank

POLYGONACEÆ.
Polygonum viviparum   Feizor
Rumex aquaticus   Helwith Moss

THYMELACEÆ.
Daphne laureola   (planted) Feizor
    mezereon   do.   do.

EMPETRACEÆ.
Empetrum nigrum   Helwith Moss
Euphorbia exigua   Common

URTICACEÆ.
Parietaria officinalis   Bolton
Humulus Lupulus   Giggleswick

AMENTIFEREÆ.
Salix pentandra   Giggleswick
    viminalis
    nigricans
    repens
    &c., &c, &c.

CONIFERÆ.
Juniperus communis   Moughton
Taxus baccata   Gordale, &c.

ORCHIDACEÆ.
Listera cordata   Ryeloaf
Epipactis latifolia   Giggleswick
    palustris   Stackhouse
Orchis ustulata   Settle
    ·latifolia   Common
Gymnadenia conopsea   Giggleswick
    albida
Habernaria latifolia   Helwith Moss
    viridis   Giggleswick
Ophrys apifera   Skipton
    muscifera   Settle
Cypripedium calceolus   Arncliffe

LILIACEÆ.
Allium Scorodoprasum   Kilnsey
    oleraceum   Feizor
    vineale   Giggleswick
Convalaria majalis   Settle
Polygonatum multiflorum   Calton
    officinale

TRILLIACEÆ.
Paris quadrifolia   Frequent

MELANTHIACEÆ.
Colchicum autumnale   Giggleswick

ALISMACEÆ.
Triglochin palustre   Cockit Moss

NAIADACEÆ.
Potamogeton densus   Ribble
    pectinatus   do.
    crispus   do.
    perfoliatus   do.
    natans   do.

JUNCACEÆ.
Juncus glomeratus   Common
    effusus   do.
    lamprocarpus   do.
    squarrosus   do.
Luzula sylvatica   do.
    campestris   do.
Narthecium ossifragum   Ingleboro'

CYPERACEÆ.
Schænus nigricans   Ingleton
Blysmus compressus   Giggleswick
Scirpus sylvaticus   Settle
Eriphorum vaginatum   Giggleswick
    polystachion   do.
Carex divisa   Settle
    pulicaris   do.
    stellulata   do.
    ovalis   do.
    curta   do.
    remota   do.
    intermedia   do.
    teretiuscula
    vulgaris
    flava   Settle
    pallescens   do.
    fulva   do.
    binervis   do.
    lævigata   do.
    panicea   do.
    strigosa
    sylvatica   do.
    pendula   do.
    præcox   do.
    hirta   do.
    ampullacea   do.
    vesicaria   do.
    paludosa ?
    riparia ?

GRAMINEÆ.

Phalaris arundinacea	
Milium effusum	
Agrostis alba	Giggleswick
Arundo phragmites	do.
Sesleria cœrulea	Giggleswick Scar
Aira flexuosa	Common
caryophylla	do.
Avena alpina	Settle
pubescens	do.
flavescens	do.
Triodia decumbens	do.
Kœleria cristata	do.
Melica uniflora	Giggleswick
nutans	do.
Molinia cœrulea	do.
Catabrosa aquatica	do.
Poa alpina	Ingleborough
pratensis	
nemoralis	Giggleswick
Briza media	Common
Cynosurus cristatns	Common
Dactylis glomerata	do.
Festuca ovina	do.
duriuscula	do.
pratensis	do.
loliacea	do.
Bromus giganteus	do.
asper	do.

Triticum caninum	do.
Nardus stricta	do.

FILICES.

Ceterach officinarum	Malham Rocks
Polypodium Phegopteris	Clapham
Dryopteris	Giggleswick
calcareum	Settle
Allosurus crispus	Fountains Fell
Cystopteris fragilis	Common
Polystichum lonchitis	Settle
aculeatum	Ingleboro'
Lastrea Oreopteris	Giggleswick
rigida	Ingleborough
Asplenium viride	Giggleswick Scars
Adiantum-nigrum	Ingleton
Botrychium lunaria	Giggleswick
Ophioglossum vulgatum	Stackhouse

LYCOPODIACEÆ.

Lycopodium clavatum	Ingleboro'
alpinum	do.
Selago	do.
Selaginella	
Selaginoides	
Equisetum palustre	Common
limosum	Ribble Bank
variegatum	Swarthmoor

CHAPTER XV.

Dialect of Craven.*

AS the subject of Dialects is an interesting one, and that of Craven has decided claims on an Anglo-Saxon origin, and is unusually free from mere slang, a cursory review of it may not improperly find a place in this volume.

The tourist will meet with oral specimens in the peculiar intonation which no orthography can convey, and as the usual dialect specimens in the form of dialogues can hardly be redeemed from the charge of vulgarity, a short specimen and a selected list only of some of the words and phrases may suffice.

The late Rev. Wm. Carr, of Bolton, an enthusiast in every thing relating to Craven, says, "I am more and more convinced that my native language is not the contemptible slang and patois which the refined inhabitants of the southern part of the kingdom are apt to consider it; but that it is the language of crowned heads, of the Court, and of the most eminent English Historians, Divines, and Poets of former ages." That there is some truth in this statement is shown by the readiness with which most Craven words may be derived from the Anglo-Saxon and other Germanic languages, and their constant recurrence in such authors as Gawin Douglas, Chaucer, Gower, Lydgate, and early Elizabethan Poets.

Although the natives of Lancashire claim for their dialect a Saxon origin, the peculiarly pastoral character of Craven, and its freedom from an excess of manufacturing population argue in favour of the antiquity and purity of its dialect, and there is certainly more of euphony iu the Craven than in the open-

* From Howson's Guide.

mouthed dialect of Lancashire. In the district ranging from Halifax to Colne, at Howarth, and Heptonstall, the one insensibly merges into the other; and again in the valley of Dent,* towards Sedbergh and Hawes, the Craven gradually assimilates itself to the Westmoreland dialect.

Dr. Whittaker makes the curious suggestion that the two nerthern scholars of Strother, whom Chaucer has made the subject of his Reeves Tale, sprang from Langstrothdale, and says that their dialect, evidently not the language of the author, is precisely the modern dialect of Craven, thus:—

> "Our Manciple I hope he will be *dede*,
> Swa werkes aye the wanges in his *hede*,
> And therefore *is I* come and eke Alayn,
> We pray you spede us *heme* in that *ye* maye."

"*I is* full swift as a *Raa*."
"He shall not *nat* skape us *bathe*."
"Why ne hadst thou put the Capel in the *Lathe*."

And Whittaker adds that he is inclined to believe the story a real one, or at least that Chaucer had heard the dialect of Alan and John in Solere Hall.

Horne Tooke remarks that Gawin Douglas's language, though written a century after Chaucer, must yet be esteemed more ancient; even as the present English speech in Scotland is in many respects more ancient than that spoken so far back as the reign of Queen Elizabeth. So Casaubon says of his time, "The Scottish language is purer than the English of the present day," where by "purer" he means nearer to the Anglo-Saxon.

As a specimen of the continual occurence of Craven words, phrases, and pronunciation in Douglas, note this passage in his preface:

> "Thocht *sum wald sware* that I the text have varyit,
> Or that I have this volume quite miscaryit,
> Or *threpe* planelie that I come *never nere hand* it,
> Or that the werk is werst that ever I *fand* it.
> Be not *ouer* studious to spy *ane* mote in myn *E*."

Further quotations from the same author will be found in the following brief list of Craven words:

NEIF. A fist. Islandic, Nefi.
> "Give me your *neif*, Monsieur Mustard Seed."—
> *Midsummer Night's Dream.*

*In the VII Vol. of the Doctor an excellent specimen of the Dent dialect is given, entitled "A Wonderful Story ot Terrible Knitters ee Dent."

FAIN. Glad. A.S., Feagn.
"For which they were as glad of his commyng,
As foule is faine when the sonne upryseth."—*Chaucer*.

MELL. Meddle. Fr., Meler. Frequent in *Spenser*, &c.
MAAR. More. Pure Dutch. A.S., Mare.
AN. If. *An* is imperative of A.S. Anan, to give, as *if* is imperative of Gifan, to give. "*An* you had an eye you might see more detraction at your heels than fortunes before you."—*Twelfth Night*. "*An* I take the humour of a thing once, I am like your tailor's needle, I go through."—
Ben Jonson.
GANG. To go. A.S., Gangan. Gang-day, Rogation Day. Hence also Gangway in a ship.
ISTEEAD ON. Instead of. Danish, Istœden. A.S., Stede, a place. Commonly in composition as gap-steead, door-steead, fire-steead, &c. Of an obstinate fellow, "He'll gang through if t'King's it gapsteead."
VARRA. Very. Fr., vrai. Anciently written veray, both in French and English.
SCUNNER. Dislike. A.S., Ascunian, to shun.
MACKLY and AHMACKLY. Most likely. A.S., Macan, to make, and Lic, like, the origin of the adverbial affix, ly. Likely in A.S. would be Liclic, hence they say "*Better an like*," Better than likely. Thus also their "*Goodlike*" is purer Saxon than Goodly.
WAE WORTH YE. Woe be to you. A.S., Weorthan, which in Anglo-Saxon and English is incorporated with Beon, to be.

"Wo worth the fayre gem vertulesse,
Wo worth that herbe that doth no bote,
Wo worth the beaute that is ruthlesse,
Wo worth that wight *trede* eche under fote."—*Chaucer*.

KNAW. To know. A.S., Cnawan.
EFTER. After. A.S., Œfter.
ALD. Old. A.S., Eald. Hence local names, Aldgate, Aldstone, &c.
BIGG. To build. A.S., Byogan. Occurs in Chaucer.
BRAAD. *Ye braad o' me*. You are like me, *i.e.*, you are of the same breed as me. A.S., Brœden.
KNOLL. To ring a funeral bell. A.S., Cnyllan. Hence also Knell. Toll, absurdly derived from Tollo, is a corruption of Knoll.
BAUK. A beam. Teutonic, Balcke.

BEEAL. To cry out. A.S., Bœl, Grief. In Chaucer.
ESH. The ash. Teutonic, Esche.
ASK. Dry. Perhaps from Teutonic, Ascha, Ashes.
TAK UNCUTH. To take offence. A.S., Uncuth, strange, unusual, uncouth. Of a cross child, "Tothers hes been good uns maks us tak uncuth at it."
WALLOW. Insipid. A.S., Walgen, to loathe.
PODDISH. A slight corruption of pottage, not porridge. Fr., Potage. "Poddish is wallow bout saut."
RIGGING. A roof. A.S., Wrigan, to cover.
SWOP. To exchange. A.S., Swipan, to sweep; where by consent of the parties each sweeps off his share.
SCALE. To spread. A.S., to divide or separate. "I shall tell you a pretty tale. It may be you have heard it, but since it serves my purpose, I will venture to *scale* it a little more."—*Coriolanus.*
ELSE. Short for Alice. Curiously enough the English word "else" is in like manner contracted from the ancient Alyse, Alys, Alles, Elles.
PLEEAN. To complain. A.S., Pleah, a plea.
CLEM. To hunger. A.S., Clemian.
YEAT. A gate. A.S., Geat. G in Anglo-Saxon was indifferently pronounced as G or Y
YOWL. To howl. Gyllan. (*See Yeat above*). Howl is as likely to have sprung from this source as from the Latin Ululo.
NESH. Tender, squeamish. A.S., Nescian, to soften.
KITLING. Kitten. Ling, a Saxon diminutive.
LEET. Light. A.S,, Leaht.
KITTLE. An inversion of "tickle."
TEW. To plague, to weary. A.S., Tawian, to tug.
AUMRY. Shady. Fr., Ombre.
OUT. Ought, anything. A.S., Awhit. "Too mich of owt's good for nowt."--*Craven Proverb.*
MUCK. Dirt, A.S., Meox. "Better hev a bairn wi' a mucky faace an wesh it nooas off."—*Craven Proverb.*
BOOK. Bulk. "'Bout book o' my neif." L not sounded, as in balk, walk, &c. "Buick" in Scotland.
"Your tender *buick* I *happit* warm,
Wi' a' a mither's care."

SHIPPON. A cow-house. From sheep-pen. Shipin in Chaucer.
SAGE. G, hard. To saw. A.S., Saga.
SHOG. To ride at a slow trot without rising in the stirrups. From Shock, and perhaps more correct than jog.

OUTSHUT. An outbuilding. A.S., Scythan, to throw forward. "Some folks hes lile brains, and some's an outshut," *i.e.*, an additional department for brains.—*Craven Proverb*. Hence also the expression, "To get shut of," is as correct as "To get quit of."

INSENSE. To enlighten. An expressive word and of obvious derivation.

SPEAN. Wean. Perhaps from Spoon.

STICKLEBUTT. Immediately, quickly. As swiftly as an arrow piercing the butt, or mark. When the bow was the Saxon's weapon, every village had its practising ground, with two raised mounds on which the butts were placed; and how commonly we find, to this day, a place in or about a village called the "Butts." Horton, Clapham, &c.

PRYALL and RYALL. Three together. A corruption of Triad.

HAIT. Hot. A.S., Hat. "Hait as fyre."—*Douglas*.

LEE. A lie. "That war ane manifest lee."—*Douglas*. "If leein wor choking thear'd be hard gasping."—*Craven Proverb*.

BE. By. It was anciently written indifferently Be or By.

FLITE. To scold. A.S., Flytan. "Qua cannot hald thare pece are fre to flite."—*Douglas*.

SILE. To strain, as milk. A.S., Syl, filth.

HULL. A small building. Goth., Hulgan, to cover.

WHITTLE. To cut sticks. From the instrument, Whittle. A.S., Hwytel, a knife.

QUARRIL. A pane of glass. Fr., Quarreau.

PARLOUS. Perilous. "By'r Lakin a parlous fear."—*Midsummer Night's Dream*. Most commonly used with tale or speech, in which case it may be parless, peerless.

TINE. To shut. A.S., Tinian.

FEST. To send out, or bind as an apprentice. A.S., Fœst, fixed.

FET. Fit. Hence Fettle, to mend.

SCHOO. She. A.S., Seo.

"Albane
Scho did behald amyd the fieldis plane."—*Douglas*.

WHARFRA. Wherefrom.

"His feris lukis about on every side,
To see quarfra the grounding dart did glide."—*Douglas*.

LIEF. Have rather. A.S., Leof, participle of Lufian, to love.

"I had as lief not be, as live to be in awe
Of such a thing as I myself."—*Julius Cæsar*.

WICK. Alive. A.S., Cwic.

TAAH. Toe. A.S., Ta.
LIG. To lie. A.S., Liegan.
STAG. A young horse. A.S., Stigan, to ascend. Coming on, as the farmers say.
STIDDY. An anvil. A.S., Stœdig, firm, fixed.
STIRK. A young heifer. A.S., Stirc.
BOUT. Without. *See Poddish.* A.S., Be-utan, be out. *But* is the same word, and now corruptly used for the ancient Bot, from Botan.

"Bot thy werke shall endure in laude and glorie,
But spot or falt condigne eterne memorie."—*Douglas.*

FAUT. Fault. Fr., Faute.
GUILEVAT. Vessel in which beer is left to ferment. Perhaps from Gill, the Ground Ivy, *Glechoma hederacea*, a plant formerly much used in domestic brewing. Apropos of the word, a Craven Fable may close this little dissertation on Craven words.

T'MOUSE I 'T GUILEVAT.

Ane day thear wor a mouse tumell'd intut guilevat, an t'cat sat a watchin on't. When it wor like to drown, it ses tut cat, "If thou'l help me out, an let me shak mesel, thou's he' mah." Saah t'cat agreead, an helpt it out, bud t'mouse ran off to it hole. Ses t'cat, I thowt thou sed I mun he' thah." "Hei!" says t'mouse wi' a gurn, "*Bud folk ses owt when ther i' drink.*"

Dr. Whittaker regrets that he was not able to retrieve any remains of traditionary poetry written by natives of Craven. "Their country," he says, "was romantic, their manners pastoral, and their dialect poetical." There are a few remains of the kind current, but they are mere doggerel, and yet there is no doubt but that approaching so nearly as it does to the Scottish, the Craven dialect might be a proper vehicle for the ballad, or the pastoral song, after the manner and the metres of the immortal Burns.

The following may serve as specimens.

TO A COVEY OF MOORGAME.

Iz't fear o' me at maks ye spring
Wi' sich a fearful flap ot' wing?
My bonny brood!
Lig saaf ith' beald ot' greenest ling,
Yer dainty food.

I'ze ower fond o' life mesell,
An freedom too, to gang an fell
   The likes o' ye;
But thear's a day at I can tell,
   When mooargam dee.

Whent' murdrous gun wi' sullen boom,
Shall send ye tul an eearly doom,
   An ye's be med
To lig it' spooartsman's bag, ith' room
   Ov heather bed.

It izn't lang sin first ye fand
Ther wings wad lift ye frae the land,
   Toth' realms ov air;
An soon ye'll fynd at shutter's hand
   Al wound 'em sair.

Gay soon yer e'en nae mair sall greet
The dewy morning's misty leet,
   Ont' mooarland wide:
An ye sall gang nae mair at neet
   Ith' ling to hide.

In vain when cruel foes ye've kent,
Ye'll trembling steal along the bent,
   Or cower ith' bog:
Wi' a' yer ways they're weel acquent,
   Baith man an dog.

Thear's lambs at's killed wi't butcher's knife,
An ducks bith' hand oth' farmer's wife
   Are doomed to dee:
Ye're favoured seur, to lose your life
   Bith' Quality.

Bud od ye now, an dooant be flaad,
I izn't ane ot' sporting traad,
   To hunt ye down;
I'ze nobbut luk whar ye wor laid,
   An then I'ze boun.

TO THE CRICKET.

Ye gamsome louper, what inspires ye
 Wi' yer feckless chirping sang?
The dreest iv'ning nivver tires ye,
 And the neet-watch ne'er is lang.

Is't prompted be domestic joyance,
 An the hearthstaan ken'd saa weel?
Or cos ye fear nae cold's annoyance,
 Nor the girds o' clemming feel?

It's said ye're linked wi' ties mysterious
  To the haam ye lang frequent,
An nowt can happen, gay er serious,
  Bud ye're gifted weel to ken't.

I'd fain believe it ;—mair betoken,
  Iv'ning hours ye love the best,
When words of household love outspoken
  Lull the jarring thowt to rest.

Ah ! lile ye mak o't sun's bright peeping
  Through the oppen kitchen door,—
Ye're ligging warm, an snugly sleeping
  Underneath the kitchen floor.

Bud twileet comes and shadows flicker
  On the snodly whitewesh'd wa' ;
An then ye wakken wick and wicker,
  An yer merry playmates ca'.

Then ower is a' the household stirring,
  Then yer chirping sangs are rife,
An chime wi't clock, and 't cat low purring,
  An the voice o' bairn or wife.

Oh ! could these haamly sounds sae quiet
  Break upon the wanderer's ear,
I' loneso e haunts, or scenes o' riot,
  Seur they co' the starting tear.

They'd bring to mind i' tones o' sadness,
  A' the lang-forgotten past,
The joys o' haam, and childhood's gladness,
  An the time o' parting last.

As a further illustration of the dialect of the Craven district we give a poetical sketch from the popular little volume "Poems in the Craven Dialect by Tom Twisleton," the third edition of which may be had from the publisher of this Guide.

HUSBAND AND WIFE;

OR, "WHARIVVER HEV YE BEEN?"

Wife.

WHARIVVER hev ye been to, ye maupin' owd tyke?
For ye've grown sich a trail-tripe, I nivver saw 't like;
An' here I've bin waitin', expectin' ye soon,
An' t' supper's bin ready an hour an' aboon.
But it's just like ye men—I declare ye've naa thowt :
This tooast 's bin by t' fire till it's pined fair to nowt—
When ye'll come yan can't tell, if ye're nobbut yance gaan ;
An' this tea 's bin i' t' pot whal it 's cowd as a staan.

There's naa gittin' a meal at reight time au through t' day,
For as true as I's here, ye're allus away.
There's nae puttin' up wi't, ye're grown sich a ganger;
But I've med up my mind 'at I'll stand it naa langer.

Husband.

Now, praytha wisht Betty—don't mak sich a din!
Thou macks t' house like a Bedlam when a boddy comes in;
It's naabody's neck if yan be rayther laat,
I'm sewer it's nowt that need set thee agaat.
I met wi' our Tommy a-gangin' past t' Ploo,
An' we caud in an' gat an odd dobbin or two;
An' wi' talkin' ower t' markets, an' farmin' an' stock,
I gav it na thowt whal it struck ten o'clock';
When I sed, "Is that ten? I mun gang reight away,
Or our owd woman 'll hev summat to say."
Saa I tuck up my glass, an' I drunk what was in it,
An' I com out o' t' house i' less 'an a minute.
Thou's hed nowt to do nobbut sit at thy eease,
Saa let it drop, Betty; now do, if ta pleease!

Wife.

Let it drop? nay, nut I—it wad mack ought fair mad,
Ye're grown just as rakish as ony young lad.
Ye may say what ye will, I declare it's a shaam
That an owd man like ye cannot stop maar at haam;
Owt 't ye hev to do, ye mud do whal its leet,
An' not stop out trailin' whal this time o' t' neet.
Ye keep me up waitin' here times withont end,
An' ye grow warse an' warse, 'stead a tryin' to mend;
But if I sud hev ye mich ofter to tell,
I'll to bed, an' I'll leave ye to fend for yersel.

Husband.

Now, Betty, my lass, do praytha be quiet!
For thou drives sich a noise, an' thou macks sich a riot,
Fooaks comin' down t' street 'll hear ivvrything plain,
An' they'll say 'at yon two's agaat differin' again.
For thou talks sich a height, thou yowls, and thou squeeaks,
Yan mud hear thee a mile an' a hauf when ta speeaks.
When yan does come haam quiet, it wad be a capper
If thy tongue didn't gang just like a bell-clapper.
But next time I'se out, now just let nowt be said,
Git thy supper at t' time, an march off to bed;
I can do varra weel be mesel, I don't doubt it;
If I can't mack my supper, I'll e'en do without it.

Wife.

That's just what yan gits when yan's done all yan can;
They're weel 'at's not pestered at au wi' a man,—
Yan may sit up an' bother, an' niver na eease,
An' when yan's done au yan nivver can pleease.
Ye think yan sud humble whativver ye say,
But I tell ye owd lad, at ye'll see different play.

But I'll off to bed, for its time I war thaar;
If ye sit up an' grummle au neet, I don't caar.
Whativver ye do, ye think yan sud say nowt;
But I tell ye, owd lad, 'at ye'll finnd yer mistack out!

Husband.

Ay! praythee be gangin'; git out o' me seet!
An' don't stand thaar preeachin' an' talkin' au neet!
Look as foul as ta likes, I don't caar a pin,
I'se just suit mysel what time I coo in.
What occasion hes thou to set up thy faace?
Thee mind thy awn business, an' keep thy awn plaace!
If I hedn't gone out it wod just a bin t' saam,
For thou's nivver at eeas when I do stop at haam.
Thou's allus at grummle, thy tongue's nivver still!
I's fair stoad wi' t' sound, an' it seems thee reight ill.
But yan needn't expect mich plezzure o' life,
When yance yan gits teed to an ill-temper'd wife;
An' to allus put up wi' yer queerness an' scorn,
It wad fair mack a chap wish 'at he'd nivver bin born.

Wife.

Nay, praya now drop it! for I've heeard quite enough,
An' rayther too mich o' that senseless stuff.
I think 'at ye've said near enough about me,
An' I's sure I's not hauf as ill-natured as ye;
For ye gang out, an' stop out, here hour efter hour,
An' then ye come haam saa surly and sour;
If yan say hauf a word 'at ye don't want to hear,
Ye're as crabbed as a wasp, an' ye growl like a beear.
It wad seem ye as weel if ye left yer ill-nature'
Whar ye gat au yer drink, ye ill-temper'd cratur!
But thaar ye'll be pleasant wi' au 'at ye see,
An' come haam an' bring yer ill-natur' to me;
If I say hauf a word i' my ahn self-defence,
Ye storm like a madman, an' talk wi' na sense.
But say what ye will, an' do au ye can,
I'll nivver be trod under foot wi' a man!
An' t' next time ye gang, au 'at I hev to say,
Is, "come haam better temper'd, or else bide away."
Ye needn't to think I's be ill off about ye;
If ye nivver come back, I can put on without ye

ADVERTISEMENTS.

The Craven Machine Printing Works,

HENRY GORE,

MERCANTILE AND FAMILY STATIONER,

BOOKSELLER, BOOKBINDER,

AND

ACCOUNT BOOK MANUFACTURER.

NEW FOUNTS OF TYPE will be added from time to time and special attention given to the production of every description of work.

In Black, Gold, and Silver, and Coloured Inks.

Reports, Tracts, Pamphlets, Lectures, Essays, &c., and the Publication of Books undertaken and issued with great care.

Relief Stamping and Die Sinking

executed with despatch at London prices.

ACCOUNT BOOKS of every description Ruled, Printed and Bound to order.

Newspapers, Periodicals, and Magazines

Supplied and Advertisements inserted in the London and Provincial Papers.

A Monthly List of NEW BOOKS and New Editions will be issued monthly and forwarded by post on application.

New Street and Duke Street, SETTLE.

ADVERTISEMENTS.

SETTLE.

LION HOTEL

Proprietor = Henry Armistead

This is the Oldest and Principal

FAMILY & COMMERCIAL HOTEL

AND POSTING HOUSE

In the district of North Craven, and is replete with every comfort at moderate charges.

COFFEE ROOM, PRIVATE SITTING ROOMS.

COMFORTABLE BEDS.

Choice Wines, Spirits, & Cigars.

WAGGONETTES, BROUGHAMS, LANDAU,

And other Conveyances.

Omnibus meets all Trains at Giggleswick Station.

ADVERTISEMENTS.

JOHN WRAY,
Auctioneer and Appraiser,
WHOLESALE AND RETAIL

HAY, STRAW AND POTATOE DEALER,

HART'S HEAD HOTEL, GIGGLESWICK.

AGENT FOR

W. ASPDEN'S, (Morecambe,) BONE MANURES.

THOS. ALTHAM
(LATE G. HIMSWORTH,)

GENERAL AND
FAMILY GROCER,
MARKET PLACE,

SETTLE.

FAMILY ORDERS CARRIAGE PAID.

Buck Hotel, Malham.

Proprietor   -   JOHN BENSON.

This House having lately been re-built is now one of the most commodious in the district.

WELL-FURNISHED SITTING AND BED ROOMS.
A LARGE ROOM FOR DINNER PARTIES.

Any number can be met with conveyances at either Bell Busk or Hellifield Station on rececipt of short notice.

POSTAL ADDRESS, MALHAM, BELL BUSK, VIA LEEDS.

THE COMMERCIAL HOTEL,
SETTLE.

THOMAS HARGREAVES, Proprietor.

TOURISTS AND COMMERCIAL GENTLEMEN

Will find excellent accommodation at the above Hotel, at moderate charges.

Comfortable Beds. Liquors of the finest qualities.

HORSES & CONVEYANCES.

John Metcalfe,
Auctioneer & Valuer,
SETTLE,

Begs to inform Farmers and the Public generally, that he is prepared to conduct with accuracy any of the following

SALES BY AUCTION

On satisfactory terms;

HOUSEHOLD FURNITURE, FARM STOCK, LANDED AND HOUSE PROPERTY.

Prompt attention will be given to all orders with which he may be favoured.

ADVERTISEMENTS.

Armistead & Shepherd,
Chemists, Druggists,
AND
FAMILY GROCERS,
SETTLE.

A. & S. have always in stock

SCHWEPPE'S AERATED WATERS,

CUFF'S LEMONADE, SODA, & POTASS WATERS,
In Syphons.

BECKETT'S FRUIT SYRUPS.

ROSE'S LIME JUICE & LIME JUICE CORDIAL,

Crosse and Blackwell's

JAMS, JELLIES, SOUPS, &c.,

Huntley & Palmer's Biscuits,
AND
GROCERIES
of every description.

PERFUMES, BRUSHES, SPONGES, and all
TOILET REQUISITES.

Physicians' Prescriptions and Family Recipes
Carefully prepared with Genuine Drugs.

PATENT MEDICINES
In stock or procured on the shortest notice.

ROBERT GRIME,

SPECIALITIES IN

School & Church Furniture

DESKS AND SEATS

With Reversible Tops, forming Backed Seats; Desk and Seat; Table and Seat, the Seat falling back making passage to walk without stepping over.

Easels, Black Boards, Drawing Boards, Masters' Desks, Tables, Benches.

ESTIMATES GIVEN FREE OF CHARGE FOR ALL CLASSES OF Buildings, House, Church, and School Furnishing.

ON THE SHORTEST NOTICE.

KIRKGATE, SETTLE.

THOMAS CLARK,
MARKET PLACE,
SETTLE.

FISH, POULTRY, & GAME
SALESMAN,

Provision and Italian Warehouseman,
FLOUR, MEAL, AND PROVENDER.

FRESH GERMAN BARM every Monday & Thursday.

Wholesale Agent for

MYER'S ROYAL CATTLE SPICE,
P. W. BARR'S DOG BISCUITS,
CARR & Co. & PEEK FREAN'S BISCUITS,
TERRY & SON'S CRAVEN & OTHER SWEETS,
CROSSE & BLACKWELL'S AND
EDWARD PINK'S GOODS IN GREAT VARIETY.
LI-QUOR TEA COMPANY,
One handsome Book given with every Three Pounds.

PRICE'S, FIELD'S AND OTHER CANDLES.
BRUSHES, &c., always on hand.

A good stock of using

POTATOES, GREEN GROCERIES & FRUIT.

A large quantity of

BEDDING & WINDOW PLANTS
And other Garden Requisites.

ROYAL OAK HOTEL,
SETTLE.

J. M. BATTY,
PROPRIETOR.

WINES, SPIRITS, &c.

Of the best quality.

Every accommodation provided for Tourists in the Craven district.

HORSES AND CONVEYANCES LET OUT ON HIRE.

R. T. ELLERSHAW,
DRAPER,

LANGCLIFFE AND SETTLE,

Begs most respectfully to thank the inhabitants of Langcliffe, Settle, and the neighbourhood for their liberal patronage during the time he has been in business and to inform them that he has

OPENED A BRANCH SHOP

IN NEW STREET, SETTLE,

And hopes to be favoured with a continuance of their patronage and support.

ADVERTISEMENTS.

M. HORNER,
PORTRAIT & LANDSCAPE
Photographer,
MARKET PLACE,
SETTLE.

VIEWS OF

Settle and District, Giggleswick, Clapham, Gordale, Malham Cove, Weathercote, Thornton Foss, Catterick, Stainforth and Scaleber Fosses, Attermire, Victoria Cave, Skipton Castle, Bolton Abbey, &c,, &c.

SOLD ALSO BY

H. GORE, Bookseller, &c.,
DUKE STREET AND NEW STREET.

ADVERTISEMENTS.

To Collectors of Topographical Works
AND OTHERS.

WHITAKER'S CRAVEN,
THE HISTORY AND ANTIQUITIES OF THE
DEANERY OF CRAVEN,

In the County of York, by THOMAS DUNHAM WHITAKER, L.L.D., F.S.A., Vicar of Whalley, Lancashire. Third Edition with many additions and corrections, edited by A. W. MORANT, F.S.A., F.G.S., &c., and with chapter on the Geology, Natural History, and Pre-historic Antiquities, by L. C. MIALL, F.G.S., Professor of Biology in the Yorkshire College.

THE New Edition of this fine work contains all the old pictures and letterpress with considerable additions and corrections. The new engravings are executed by well-known artists, and the book is printed in a superior manner.

It is well known that the old edition of Whitaker rose in price to eight times its original cost and any copies on sale were the objects of keen competition.

I have a few copies left which will be offered for a short time at the published prices.

Every person who is at all interested in the district ought to possess a copy of 'Whitaker' and secure this last opportunity of obtaining one before the inevitable rise in price. As an investment alone the offer is worth consideration. The prices are—

4to cloth boards..........................	£3	3	0
4to bound half morocco, cloth sides	4	4	0
Do. do. in 2 vols., with pedigrees mounted on linen	5	5	0

HENRY GORE, Duke Street, SETTLE.

FLYING HORSE SHOE HOTEL
CLAPHAM STATION.

Henry Coates, Proprietor.

THIS HOTEL is most conveniently situated for parties who wish to explore the most romantic part of Yorkshire. The proprietor has the privilege of showing Ingleboro' Cave which is one of the greatest curiosities in the kingdom. The district abounds in attractions for the Botanist, Geologist, and lover of the beauties of nature, and a week or more may be most enjoyably spent in exploring those in the immediate neighbourhood of this Hotel.

GOOD TROUT FISHING
In the Wenning, close at hand.

HORSES, CONVEYANCES, GUIDES, &c.
FAMILIES ACCOMMODATED BY THE WEEK OR MONTH.

A BOUNTIFUL TABLE
CHOICE LIQUORS,
AND MODERATE CHARGES
ARE THE FEATURES OF THIS ESTABLISHMENT.

Trains 45 minutes from Skipton and the same from Lancaster.

Postal Address—CLAPHAM, Lancaster.

ADVERTISEMENTS.

The only Establishment in the North where 100 high class Instruments can be bought at prices commonly charged for inferior made Instruments.

Morland Brothers,

County Music Saloon,

(Opposite the Town Hall),

LANCASTER,

Are the Agents in LANCASTER, SETTLE, and neighbourhood, for Broadwood, Collard, Erard, Hopkinson, Brinsmead, and every other RELIABLE Pianoforte Maker,

Chappell, Alexandre, Trayser, Cesarini, Mason & Hamlin, Estey, Geo. Wood, and every RELIABLE Harmonium and American Organ Maker.

50 PIANOFORTES

From 20 to 150 Guineas, and

40 Harmoniums and American Organs

From 5 to 50 Guineas, for the Cottage, School, or Mansion.

Every Instrument personally selected in London.

Old Instruments taken in Exchange.

First-Class London Tuners

Visit all parts.

Repairs of every description skilfully executed.

ADVERTISEMENTS.

TO ANGLERS.

HENRY GORE,

(LATE WILDMANS)

KEEPS IN STOCK ALL VARIETIES OF

FISHING TACKLE

ARTIFICIAL FLIES 1/6 per dozen.

MINNOWS, 1/- and 1/6 each.

Tackle for Live Minnows, Worm Tackle, Reel Lines In great variety.

A GOOD SELECTION OF RODS,

From 6d. upwards.

NEW INN HOTEL,
CLAPHAM.

Tourists and Families travelling in Yorkshire will find very superior accomodation, combined with moderate charges. at this Hotel. It has recently been improved and enlarged. It is situated in the very heart of the finest scenery in Yorkshire,—the celebrated Ingleborough and Weathercote Caves, Gaping-gill Falls, &c., all being within an easy walk of the Hotel. The picturesque and romantic grounds of James Farrer, Esq., Ingleborough, to which visitors to the Hotel have access.

There is excellent Trout Fishing close to the Hotel.

Horses and Conveyances for Hire.

Special Accomodation for Pic-Nic Parties.

THOMAS SCOTT, PROPRIETOR.

Postal Address, CLAPHAM, LANCASTER.

INGLETON.

INGLEBORO' HOTEL,
COMMERCIAL & POSTING HOUSE.

This Hotel a new and stately erection is fitted up with every comfort and convenience to meet the growing wants of commercial gentlemen and visitors. It contains five spacious sitting rooms, fourteen bedrooms, coffee room, smoke rooms, bath rooms, and every other accommodation, and has lately been re-furnished and renovated.

EXCELLENT FISHING. Tickets may be had at the Hotel.

---o---

WHEAT SHEAF HOTEL

This old-established Hotel is situate in MAIN STREET, INGLETON, and affords

EXCELLENT ACCOMMODATION FOR TRAVELLERS, TOURISTS, ETC.

It has recently been greatly enlarged, several additional Sleeping and Sitting Rooms having been added to it., and is now calculated to accommodate double the number of visitors, &c., that it has heretofore done.

There is also a large and capacious BILLIARD ROOM attached.

It has for upwards of half a century had the reputation of being one of the best conducted Commercial Hotels in the West Riding of Yorkshire.

POST HORSES, TRAPS, CARRIAGES, WAGONETTES &c.

The above Hotels are only about 100 yards apart and within three minutes walk from the railway station.

Proprietor - *T. REDMAYNE.*

Ingleton is situated almost in the centre of a beautiful, romantic, and salubrious district, within one hour's walk from the summit of Ingleborough.

It affords excellent fishing, trout, &c.—the rivers Doe and Greta flowing through the village.

It is within easy distance of the mountains Whernside and Pennyghent; also the Natural Caves—Weathercote, Yordas, Bruntscar, Douk Cave, Hurtle-pot, Jingle-pot, and other Caves in the beautiful valley of Chapel-le-dale.

Thornton Force and the beautiful waterfalls and romantic scenery of Beazley may be reached in half-an-hour's walk.

All lovers of natural curiosities may spend many weeks in visiting the romantic scenery in this district.

ADVERTISEMENTS.

Settle Cave Exploration.
VICTORIA CAVE.

The results already achieved are before the public in the reports of the British Association, in Professor Boyd-Dawkins work on "Cave-Hunting," in the Geological portion of a new edition of "Whitaker's History of Craven," by Professor L. C. Miall, and in other works.

The great interest in the Victoria Cave lies in the long succession of events represented by its contents, which are of the greatest importance to the historian, the antiquary, and the geologist. The bearing of some of the facts elicited is still under discussion. but briefly the general results may be described as follows—The fine collections made here and deposited in the Museum of Giggleswick School illustrate the occupation of the country and of the cave at intervals, by the early English, Roman, and Celtic populations ; then further back by many ages are found the remains of people who used the newer type of stone implements. In beds of earlier age we have evidence of the occupation of Yorkshire by the reindeer and the grisly bear in times immediately succeeding and probably preceding the development of a great ice-sheet in the north of England. Still further back we are enabled to decipher the record of a remotely distant age when man was living on the same ground with the great cave-bear, the hyæna, elephant, rhinoceros, hippopotamus, bison, and other animals. The cave is unique in possessing data showing the existence of man in the North of England *before* these cold conditions came on which covered the Northern Counties with a thick mantle of ice.

The LANCASTER GUARDIAN
ESTABLISHED 1837.   PRICE 1d.

The *Guardian* is distinguished by the accuracy and fulness of its LOCAL REPORTS, by its complete record of DISTRICT INTELLIGENCE, and it seeks to keep its readers well informed on the POLITICAL, GENERAL, and LITERARY NEWS OF THE WEEK.

TO ADVERTISERS.—Having been established over 40 years, the *Guardian* has gained a very eminent position as a Family Newspaper and an influential medium for Advertisements   Its circulation has now so largely increased in all directions, and amongst all classes, that it has been recognised as THE BEST ADVERTISER in North Lancashire, the adjoining districts of Westmorland and the West Riding of Yorkshire, and particularly in Lunesdale, Craven and Ribblesdale.

The *Guardian* is issued at an earlier hour on Friday, in order to permit its despatch by the afternoon trains, but subsequent editions will be issued when required by the arrival of Later News and Local Reports.

Guardian Office, Church Street, Lancaster.

ADVERTISEMENTS.

OF ALL DESCRIPTIONS

IN EVERY VARIETY OF STYLE,

WITH DESPATCH.

Ledgers, Journals, Day Books, Time Books, Cheque Books, &c.,
Ruled to pattern, with printed headings, and bound to order.

HENRY GORE,
BOOKBINDER, MACHINE RULER, &c.,
DUKE STREET, SETTLE.

POEMS

IN THE

CRAVEN DIALECT

BY TOM TWISLETON.

THIRD EDITION; WITH AN ADDENDUM,

CONTAINING

Poems by Henry L. Twisleton.

Paper covers, 1/–; cloth, limp, 1/6.

HENRY GORE, Bookseller, &c., SETTLE.

ADVERTISEMENTS.

HOT-AIR STOVES.

Messrs. RIMINGTON & SON,
ENGINEERS & IRON-FOUNDERS,
CRAVEN IRON WORKS, SKIPTON, YORKSHIRE,

Beg most respectfully to inform the Clergy and the Public that they are prepared to fix their much approved system of

HOT-AIR STOVES,

Which has been used in upwards of 1,000 Churches, Chapels, Schools, and Private Residences, at a Moderate Cost.

MOST UNDENIABLE REFERENCES CAN BE FURNISHED OF THOSE NOW IN WORKING, AND PERFECT SUCCESS GUARANTEED.

TERMS TO BE KNOWN ON APPLICATION.

TESTIMONIALS.

Lavington, August 29th.

Sir,—I have much pleasure in bearing my testimony to the effectual and economical manner in which the stoves you have placed in different churches in my diocese have warmed; and also to add that they are free from the objection of unsightliness which is fatal to so many modes of warming churches.
To Mr. W. Rimington.
I am very truly yours, S. OXON.

Abingdon, Jan. 17th, 1879.

Messrs. Rimington supplied the heating apparatus to the large church of S. Helens, Abingdon, when it was restored in the year 1873. The church presented great difficulties which Messrs. Rimington successfully overcame. We have much pleasure in certifying that, in our opinion, the method of warming adopted in this case was very efficient and successful,
ALFRED POTT, Archdeacon, Vicar.
SLADE J. BAKER, Churchwarden.
This church contains about 270,000 cubic feet of air, and has many large windows.

Abingdon, Jan. 18th, 1879.

Dear Sir,—As my co-Churchwarden is dead, I have added my name to the testimonial signed by the late Vicar. I do so with much pleasure as I am thoroughly well satisfied with your method of warming churches. St. Helen's is a very difficult building to heat, as it is very large and contains five aisles. For the two winters I was in office I did not have a complaint of the church being cold. After receiving your instructions, I personally undertook the working of the stoves, and my experience gave me the very best results. I found that by lighting up at five I could get the church well warmed by ten with sufficient heat to last till night. I discovered that the consumption of fuel was not very large when the fires were well alight, bright and clear, a small quantity of coal added at intervals generated the largest amount of heat, taking care that the plates did not get red hot. They never smoked or gave off any offensive smell, and are at the present time in good working order. I am fully satisfied of the efficiency of your apparatus if proper attention is paid to matters of detail, such as looking to the pilot stove and keeping the fires bright, and not adding large quantities at a time.
Yours truly, SLADE J. BAKER, late Churchwarden.
To Messrs. Rimington & Son, Craven Iron Works, Skipton, Yorkshire.

Cleaton Vicarage, Cleobury Mortimer, 23rd Jan., 1879.

Dear Sir,—You ask me to say what I think of your heating apparatus which I have just had fixed in my church. So far as I can judge from a short trial, (and I can see nothing to get out of order), it is the cheapest and best means of warming a church I have ever seen, and I can only wish it had been placed in the church from the very first, for it would have saved considerable expense and immense inconvenience.
Yours very truly,
GEO. P. TURNER.

Mr. Wm. Rimington, Iron Foundry,
Skipton-in-Craven, Yorkshire.

ADVERTISEMENTS.

THE Craven Herald
And WENSLEYDALE STANDARD

Is the only eight-page Newspaper, and the only Conservative organ, having a general circulation in Craven and the adjoining districts of the West Riding of Yorkshire, East Lancashire, and the borders of Westmorland.

The *Newspaper Press Directory*, the special organ of the trade, says: "The *Herald* circulates generally throughout the West Riding of Yorkshire and East Lancashire, principally in Skipton and the Craven district. Well-arranged and full reports of all occurrences in the district are given with the general intelligence of the week; special attention being given to the markets, and matters of interest to graziers, agriculturists, and landed proprietors."

The *Herald* is published on Friday afternoon in time for the evening post, and is published through its extensive district by nearly one hundred agents, in the numerous towns and populous places within the confines of Lancaster, Clitheroe, Burnley, Keighley, Otley, Harrogate, Ripon, Bedale, Richmond, and Kendal.

Although the *Herald* has a very large and influential circulation, and receives the Government and other Public and Official Notices, its scale of charges is comparatively low, being as follows: Election and Public Notices, 6d. per line; Railway Announcements, Contracts, Sales of Property by Auction or Private, 4d. per line; Entertainments and Trade Advertisements, 1s. 8d. per inch (displayed), or if ordered for a quarter 10d. per inch, for a half-year 8d. and for a year 6d. per inch, each insertion.

CRICKET MATERIALS.

HENRY GORE

Has on Sale, during the Season, a very large and well-selected Stock of

BATS, BALLS, & WICKETS,
GLOVES AND GAUNTLETS,
LEG GUARDS, BELTS, BAT COVERS,
SCORING BOOKS, AND EVERY CRICKET REQUISITE.

DARK'S AND DUKE'S BEST MATCH BALLS.
CLUBS SUPPLIED ON LIBERAL TERMS.

ADVERTISEMENTS.

TO FARMERS.

ESTABLISHED 1846.

CONCENTRATED

Blood & Bone Manure Works,

STANDISH LOWER GROUND,

NEAR WIGAN, LANCASHIRE.

WILLIAM GIFFORD,

LONG PRESTON,

Has much pleasure in informing Farmers, Agriculturists, and the public that he has been appointed by Mr. ABRAHAM LLOYD, the Proprietor of the above Works, his Agent for the sale of BOILED and RAW GROUND BONES and special

ARTIFICIAL MANURES

For every crop, and hopes to receive a share of their patronage.

These old and established Manures are well known and have been extensively used in various parts of England for many years and can therefore be recommended with confidence.

First-class references can be given amongst which the following gentlemen are selected (being residents of the Craven district) who have used the manures with most satisfactory results and who have kindly permitted reference being made to them :—Messrs. W. Todd, Kelber, Coniston; J. Wilson, Halton West; Wm. Parker, Halton West; J. & A. Bell, Otterburn; J. Winder, Gallaber, Hellifield; T. Holgate, Brooklands, Long Preston: W. Batty, Little Stainforth, Settle; W. Knowles, Kirkby Malham; H. Morphet, Wigglesworth.

W. G. has always in stock Smith's celebrated Devonshire Oils, Calf Drinks, and Foot-rot Mixtures; Theobald's Improved Driffield Oils, Cleansing and Felon Drinks for Cattle, Powders for Ill-conditioned Horses, Worms, Influenza, &c. ; the well-known Old Jimmy and Whitworth Bottles for sprains and bruises ; Castor Oil and Epsom Salts.

LICENSED DEALER IN PATENT MEDICINES.

ADVERTISEMENTS.

DUKE STREET, SETTLE.

HENRY GORE,
(Late WILDMANS,)

Has constantly in stock a large assortment of

Bibles, Prayer Books, and Church Services,
IN PLAIN AND ORNAMENTAL BINDINGS.

WESLEYAN HYMNS & SUPPLEMENT, CONGREGATIONAL HYMN BOOKS, ETC.

Any not in stock procured on the shortest notice.

Hymns Ancient and Modern, the new & revised editions,
With and without tunes, and bound with the Book of Common Prayer, in plain and elegant bindings.

THE INGLEBOROUGH CAVE.

This Cave exceeds all others in this part of the Kingdom in the variety of Stalactites & Stalagmites, Subterranean Waterfalls, Arched Gothic Roofs, Giant's Hall, &c.; the length of the latest discoveries at present reaches 1000 yards.

HENRY COATES has the privilege of shewing the Cave. Parties visiting the Inn will find every comfort and very moderate charges. A week or more might be well spent in a locality so abounding in natural curiosities.

Families accommodated with Apartments in the above-mentioned Inn by the week or month. Trout fishing in the Wenning that runs close by the Inn, and in the neighbouring streams. The Landlord is privileged to give leave to fish. Cars, Guides, Stabling, &c.

Trains—45 minutes from Skipton, and 45 from Lancaster.

All parties by rail wishing to visit the above Caves, must apply for Guides and Conveyances, if needed, to the Proprietor, at the Inn, Clapham Station, to save disappointment, as he is the only person authorised to shew them.

HENRY COATES,
Flying Horse Shoe Inn,
CLAPHAM STATION.

ADVERTISEMENTS.

BAILEY BROTHERS,
(LIMITED,)
Market Place, CLITHEROE,
Wholesale Grocers & Corn Millers,
IMPORTERS OF

Irish and American Provisions,

Will submit samples and prices to buyers on application.

They are makers of one of the best and cheapest CATTLE SPICES, one trial will prove its superiority: also B. Bros.

INDIAN STARCH FINISH
Is a great boon to the Laundry, prevents the iron sticking, and leaves a beautiful ivory finish.

PHOTOGRAPHS
OF ALL THE
PRINCIPAL OBJECTS OF INTEREST
IN THE
DISTRICT OF CRAVEN
MAY BE HAD AT
HENRY GORE'S, (late Wildmans,) SETTLE.

———o———

Cartes, 6d.; Cabinets, 1/–; mounted or unmounted.

JAMES MAUDSLEY,
Auctioneer and Valuer
Town Head Farm, LONG PRESTON.

ADVERTISEMENTS.

NOW READY, (Revised edition), 184 pp. crown 8vo. Price 2s. 6d., or post free for 32 stamps.

A SCHOOL FLORA,

FOR THE USE OF

ELEMENTARY

BOTANICAL CLASSES,

BY

W. MARSHALL WATTS, D. Sc. (Lond.)

Physical Science Master in the Giggleswick Grammar School.

———o———

LONDON:
SIMPKIN, MARSHALL, & CO.; FREDERICK WARNE & CO.
SETTLE, HENRY GORE.

1879.

PURIFIED
Country-Made Bedding.

John Tatham & Son
MAKERS OF THE

FIVE GUINEA
FEATHER BEDS.

CREAM LINEN TICK & WHITE FEATHERS
ALL THROUGH ALIKE.

Price List of Eighteen qualities of Feather Beds, &c., on application.

PURIFIED
HAIR MATTRESSES

GUARANTEED GENUINE

And free from all annoying impurities.

☞ Estimates furnished for Feather Beds, Pillows, Hair or Wool Mattresses, Flock Beds, Straw Palliasses, Blankets, Sheetings, &c., on application.

JOHN TATHAM & SON,
BEDDING WAREHOUSEMEN,
SETTLE.

www.ingramcontent.com/pod-product-compliance
Lightning Source LLC
Chambersburg PA
CBHW030308170426
43202CB00009B/922